STANFORD FRENCH AND ITALIAN STUDIES 18

An Allegory of Form

Literary Self-Consciousness in the *Decameron*

MILLICENT JOY MARCUS

ANMA LIBRI

AN ALLEGORY
OF FORM

LITERARY SELF-CONSCIOUSNESS
IN THE *DECAMERON*

STANFORD
FRENCH AND ITALIAN
STUDIES

editor

ALPHONSE JUILLAND

editorial board

JOHN AHERN

MARC BERTRAND

ROBERT GREER COHN

FRANCO FIDO

RAYMOND D. GIRAUD

PAULINE NEWMAN-GORDON

volume XVIII

ANMA LIBRI

AN ALLEGORY OF FORM

LITERARY SELF-CONSCIOUSNESS IN THE *DECAMERON*

MILLICENT JOY MARCUS

1979
ANMA LIBRI

Stanford French and Italian Studies is a collection of scholarly publications devoted to the study of French and Italian literature and language, culture and civilization. Occasionally it will allow itself excursions into related Romance areas.
Stanford French and Italian Studies will publish books, monographs, and collections of articles centering around a common theme, and is open also to scholars associated with academic institutions other than Stanford.
The collection is published for the Department of French and Italian, Stanford University by Anma Libri.

Burgess
PQ
4287
.M326

WITHDRAWN

© 1979 by ANMA LIBRI & Co.
P.O. Box 876, Saratoga, Calif. 95070
All rights reserved
ISBN 0-915838-21-4
Printed in the United States of America

ACKNOWLEDGMENTS

Boccaccio once said that without the consolations of a kind and sympathetic friend, he would never have been able to free himself from melancholy and produce the book which would, in turn, console so many others. Like Boccaccio, I owe an inestimable debt of gratitude to literary friends; and there the analogy stops. But it is nonetheless fitting that a book about the *Decameron* begin in the same way as its source does: on a note of thanks.

Perhaps my most formative literary friendship has been with Giuseppe Mazzotta, whose Yale University seminar in fall 1970 turned the *Decameron* into a rich inventory of the history of ideas. It was this class which dramatically changed my thinking about Boccaccio by revealing in his 100 tales for idle ladies a serious statement about the uses and abuses of human fictions. Much of my current approach to the *Decameron* owes its inception to this fortunate classroom experience.

In a more general sense, I would like to thank John Freccero, whose intellectual and pedagogical example inspired my own interest in teaching medieval literature; Thomas Bergin, whose devotion to Italian letters is only surpassed by his devotion to his students; and Gian-Paolo Biasin who encouraged me to begin Italian studies twelve years ago, and has been unstinting in his support ever since.

Colleagues here at the University of Texas have been the best of literary friends. Thanks go to David Armstrong, William Kibler, and especially to Wayne Rebhorn, who not only read the manuscript once, with painstaking care, but heroically offered to do so again once the revisions had been completed. I have often availed myself of his expertise, both scholarly and practical, in the preparation of the manuscript. Special thanks are also due to my colleague in Italian, Joy Potter, who generously shared with me the critical and bibliographical results of her own research on Boccaccio.

Though strangers to the world of medieval Italian literature, my parents have been intimately involved in this project from the start, sending me a scholarly edition of the *Decameron* as a gift, and making it financially possible for me to take time off from teaching to research the manuscript. Without their constant interest and help, this book would have remained in the realm of "what if."

I would like to express my deepest appreciation to Vice-President Irwin C. Lieb and to the Subsidy Committee of the Office of Graduate Studies at the University of Texas for generously supporting the publication of my manuscript. I am also grateful to Mrs. Robert Stephenson for her superb typing, to the University of Texas U.R.I. for awarding me a Special Research Grant to finance her services, plus the xeroxing of the manuscript, and to the editorial board of *Stanford French and Italian Studies* for its prompt and thorough consideration of my work. The book would be much the weaker without the benefit of the editors' excellent suggestions for revision.

The most important of my literary friends remains to be acknowledged—he is my husband and colleague, Robert Hill. By combining support with honest criticism, he has given me a sense of objectivity that alone I could never have achieved. When Boccaccio says in the proem of the *Decameron* that a dear friend helped him find the equanimity and strength to write, I know whereof he speaks.

CONTENTS

To Marion, Sydney, and Robert

INTRODUCTION

Perhaps if he had lived in another century, and not in the one dominated by Dante and Petrarch, Boccaccio would have commanded a
more just appraisal for his contribution to literary history. But instead
he is like the younger brother of illustrious siblings, standing in the
shadow of two giants whose achievements have become the yardstick
for his own very different, and hence misjudged, stamp of genius.
Although Boccaccio chose and perfected a genre utterly alien to his
two predecessors, although he took his literary inheritance in a direction distinct from theirs, critics persist in reading him as a "fallen"
Dante, as a Petrarch wanting in refinement and conscience, as an
apostate from the world of serious moral concerns. The epithet
Johannes tranquillitatum[1] testifies to a critical bias so weighed in favor of
literature with direct moralizing content that anyone who expresses
values in subtler, less obvious ways becomes an escapist, a loafer,
tranquillus. It is for this reason that critics of the stature of Erich
Auerbach and Charles Singleton find Boccaccio devoid of moral vision, lacking a "*sovrasenso* or system of hidden meanings for a key to
unlock,"[2] of a worldliness "too insecure and unsupported to serve,
after the fashion of Dante's figural interpretation, as a basis on which
the world could be ordered, interpreted, and represented as a reality
and as a whole."[3] They are only the most modern exponents of a long
tradition to which Francesco De Sanctis also gave his authoritative
stamp. "L'arte è la sola serietà del Boccaccio, sola che lo renda

---

[1] For the origin of this epithet, see Aldo Scaglione, *Nature and Love in the Late Middle
Ages* (Berkeley and Los Angeles, 1963), pp. 118-119.
[2] Charles S. Singleton, "On Meaning in the *Decameron*," *Italica*, 21 (1944), 124.
[3] Erich Auerbach, *Mimesis: The Representation of Reality in Western Literature*, trans. Willard R. Trask (Princeton, 1971), p. 231.

1

meditativo fra le orgie dell'immaginazione, e gli corrughi la fronte nella più sfrenata licenza."[4] For such critics, Boccaccio is the quintessential entertainer, the producer of art for its own sake, an aesthete whose stories "non hanno altro fine che di far passare il tempo piacevolmente, e sono veri mezzani di piacere e d'amore, il vero Principe Galeotto."[5]

De Sanctis, Singleton, Auerbach, and others[6] are looking for a Dante in Boccaccio, and when they do not find him there, disparage the storyteller in terms which have no relevance to his narrative art. What those who read Boccaccio in light of Dante fail to see is the way in which Boccaccio's literary form constitutes its own moralizing gloss. For this storyteller uses genre in such a self-conscious and conscientious way that the stories bespeak their own morality, and render unnecessary the author's direct intervention in the text. When readers are able to set aside comparisons with Dante and finally entertain the autonomy of Boccaccio's contribution, the approach which generates the misnomer *Johannes tranquillitatum* will give way to a far more serious study of the morality that Boccaccio builds into the storytelling genre itself.

Indeed we do well to consider what is new and courageous about Boccaccio, rather than what is old and unsatisfactory in relation to his literary "siblings," Dante and Petrarch. Salvatore Battaglia's study of genre history[7] gives a vivid idea of how Boccaccio transformed the medieval *exemplum*, which was relegated to the illustration of abstract truths, to the *novella*, a form capable of expressing the problematic of a changing world, free from subjugation to any external systems of interpretation. In his study of Boccaccio's prose style,[8] Auerbach shows how the storyteller creates a vernacular worthy of this newly ennobled literary form. And in the architectonic design of the *Decameron* we have further proof that Boccaccio takes this erstwhile "inferior" narrative art quite seriously.[9] By embedding the 100 tales of his collection in an elegant and noble frame story, by lavishing great care on this ordering device which contains and balances the often

---

[4] Francesco De Sanctis, *Storia della letteratura italiana* (Florence, 1965), p. 310.

[5] Ibid., p. 291.

[6] See, for example, Henri Hauvette, *Boccace: Étude biographique et littéraire* (Paris, 1914), pp. 269, 271. Though R. Hastings calls Boccaccio a moralist, he insists that didacticism takes a second place to entertainment, setting forth a hierarchy of values with which I believe Boccaccio would disagree. See *Nature and Reason in the 'Decameron'* (Manchester, 1975), p. 6.

[7] Salvatore Battaglia, *Giovanni Boccaccio e la riforma della narrativa* (Naples, 1969).

[8] See Auerbach, pp. 203-231.

[9] On the deliberateness of Boccaccio's design, specifically the internal unity of each day and the relationship of the days to the overall plan of the work, see Ferdinando Neri, "Il disegno ideale del *Decameron*," in *Storia e poesia* (Turin, 1936), p. 60.

equivocal subjects of his tales, by peopling this *cornice* with ten idealized youths who serve as internal narrators, and by casting his stories in a prose which is at once ornate and flexible, rhetorical and alive, Boccaccio is able to elevate the medieval genre of storytelling from its status as a popular mode to the heights of literary respectability.[10]

This sudden "uplifting" of genre suggests a conscious and deliberate program on Boccaccio's part to make his literary form a full-fledged thematic concern. So conspicuous is his use of the storyteller's apparatus that it becomes part of the primary subject matter of this text and proves indispensable to a complete and intelligible reading of the tales. For this reason I take issue with a second school of thematic critics who differ from the Christian figuralists, Auerbach and Singleton, in that they do not impose a Dantesque morality on Boccaccio, but consider him instead in the context of the history of ideas. Aldo Scaglione has traced this trend from De Sanctis to Branca,[11] and adds his own contribution to the polemic of medieval *versus* Renaissance by showing in Boccaccio a naturalism which prefigures the Renaissance but is nonetheless an outgrowth of medieval doctrines of realism. His study seeks to correct the unilateral and ahistorical bias of De Sanctis' naturalism "which he conceived as an essentially 'new' attitude, in direct and complete reaction against medieval spiritualism, asceticism, and mysticism"[12] by placing the *Decameron* in a historical perspective and revealing the source of Boccaccio's ideology in medieval thought. Scaglione finds the storyteller's theory of love to be in accordance with contemporary mores, for his naturalism is nothing more than a compromise between the medieval polarities of misogyny and philogyny—the dialectic generated by a puritanical Church on the one hand and the idealism of courtly love on the other.

Although Scaglione's position is a pivotal one, his remains ultimately incomplete in its absence of formal concerns. The history of ideas approach is insufficient when applied alone to the *Decameron* for it takes into account only content, and ignores the subtlety and irony of an author who uses his form to shape and determine his meaning. When taken together with considerations of genre, the history of ideas method will lead to rich and important discoveries, but alone it will limit the reader to an incomplete and literal-minded perspective.

Recent critics take the *Decameron* as a highly self-reflexive literary work, full of intra-textual commentaries on its own art. Guido Al-

[10] See De Sanctis, p. 290, and Giorgio Padoan, "Mondo aristocratico e mondo comunale nell'ideologia e nell'arte di Giovanni Boccaccio," *Studi sul Boccaccio*, II (Florence, 1964), 143.
[11] Scaglione, pp. 48-53.
[12] Ibid., p. 49.

mansi, Giuseppe Mazzotta, and Joy Hambuechen Potter[13] have all made contributions to the metaliterary study of Boccaccio's text. Taking this as the impetus for my own work, I have made narrative form a special object of study, finding in Boccaccio's manipulations of genre the very locus of meaning in the *Decameron*.

*

*   *

In his *De genealogia deorum gentilium*, the mythological compendium written after the *Decameron*, Boccaccio gives a picturesque account of what has promised to be, in less primitive terms, his own narrative vocation.

> There was never a maundering old woman, sitting with others late of a winter's night at the home fireside making up tales of Hell, the fates, ghosts, and the like—much of it pure invention—that she did not feel beneath the surface of her tale, as far as her limited mind allowed, at least some meaning—sometimes ridiculous no doubt—with which she tries to scare the little ones, or divert the young ladies, or amuse the old, or at least show the power of fortune.[14]

So vivid is this fireside scene that it temporarily eclipses the debate of the surrounding passage in Book XIV of the *De genealogia*. The reader automatically forms a mental picture of the garrulous old woman and her spellbound friends who listen open-mouthed to her yarns, their wonder propelling her on to ever more fantastic creations. But our imaginative impression does not preclude an awareness of some hidden meaning lurking "beneath the surface of her tale" which gives this scene an almost supernatural tinge.

Most intriguing is the fact that Boccaccio's archetypal storyteller is an allegorist, albeit an unconscious one who is only aware after the fact that her stories contain a kernel of hidden meaning. These tales

[13] See Guido Almansi, *The Writer as Liar: Narrative Technique in the 'Decameron'* (London, 1975); Guiseppe Mazzotta, "The *Decameron*: The Marginality of Literature," *University of Toronto Quarterly*, 42 (1972), 64-81; "The *Decameron*: The Literal and the Allegorial," *Italian Quarterly*, 18 (Spring 1975), 53-73; as well as Joy Hambuechen Potter, "Boccaccio as Illusionist: The Play of Frames in the *Decameron*," *Humanities Association Review*, 26 (Fall 1975), 327-345. M. Marti gives a meta-narrative reading of one of Boccaccio's minor works in "Per una metalettura del *Corbaccio*: Il ripudio di Fiammetta," in *Giornale storico della letteratura italiana*, 153 (1976), 60-86.

[14] *Boccaccio on Poetry, Being the Preface and the Fourteenth and Fifteenth Books of Boccaccio's 'Genealogia Deorum Gentilium,'* trans. Charles G. Osgood (New York, 1956), p. 54. This passage constitutes one of the many contradictions in Boccaccio's defense of poetry. Here he refutes his own fourth classification of fiction-writing—that is, old wives' tales—which, he says, contain no truth (see p. 49). The contradiction is a suggestive one, paradoxically strengthening his argument for the universality of fiction's didactic power, despite his earlier dismissal of the old wives' tales as meaningless.

have a life of their own, transcending the intentionality of their teller, making her an unwitting vessel of some preexistent truth. The old woman thus joins the public of her own tale as she seeks to understand its meaning along with the other listeners, surprised, along with them, at the revelation of the hidden meaning which so mysteriously unfolds.

In the example of the maundering old woman, Boccaccio makes his strongest argument against those who would read his fictions as meaningless. If this primitive storyteller unconsciously weaves hidden truths into her tales, how could we ever suspect an artist as sophisticated and self-aware as Boccaccio of composing hollow fictions? The writer uses the example of this maundering old woman as a limiting case of his own argument—if her fictions work on an allegorical level (of which she is only belatedly aware), whose would not?

I use the word allegory as Boccaccio himself does, in its broadest sense, as any meaning *other than* literal. "All these secondary meanings, by whatever name, are essentially allegorical. For 'allegory' is from ἄλλο, Latin *alienum*, and is so called being alien from the literal or historical sense."[15] Throughout this study, I will be using allegory to mean a second or hidden truth that is different from, but conveyed by, the literal vehicle of the fiction itself. In fact, it is this allegorical theory of fiction which constitutes Boccaccio's best argument against the poet-haters who accuse their enemies of superficial, frivolous, and seductive creations, ignorant as these philistines are of the deeper, allegorical meanings inherent in all fictions, from pagan mythology to the parables of Christ. Indeed, Boccaccio builds into his very definition of fiction the necessity of this twofold, allegorical reading: "Fiction is a form of discourse which, under guise of invention, illustrates or proves an idea, and, as its superficial aspect is removed, the meaning of the author is clear."[16]

Implicit in the term allegory, I find no prejudice as to the *kind* of hidden meaning to be discerned.[17] Allegory here simply means the confidence that a hidden truth underlies the literal surface and justifies it in terms that the poet-haters would not dispute. Regardless of the type of truth to be discovered, Boccaccio endorses its quest in his insistence upon the allegorical substratum of all fictions. The theory implies more a *way* of interpreting than the *end results* of that interpretation when Boccaccio condemns those who "read discursively, and of course, derive no profit from the story."[18] Boccaccio's emphasis on the

[15] Ibid., p. xviii.
[16] Ibid., p. 48.
[17] For a discussion of Boccaccio's allegorical systems, see Osgood, pp. xviii-xix.
[18] Ibid., p. 105.

built-in allegory of fictions, then, carries with it the injunction to a certain kind of reading: one that accounts for the vertical multiplication of senses as well as the horizontal sequence of narrative events. The good reader of literature will be one alert to allegory, always in search of the other possible meanings hidden beneath the pleasing veil of fiction.

In the *De genealogia*, Boccaccio insists that "poetic fiction differs from a lie in that in most instances it bears not only no close resemblance to the literal truth, but no resemblance at all; on the contrary, it is quite out of harmony and agreement with the literal truth."[19] And in the *Decameron*, we find a similar, though implied, pronouncement in the strict division between history and fiction[20] with which the frame story begins. Here, Boccaccio immediately discourages any literal-minded interpretation of the text by asserting the historical inauthenticity of his narrative venture. As the author moves from his prefatory pages on the history of the Black Plague to the frame story itself, he reveals the irreconcilable difference between "the literal truth" on the one hand and "poetic fiction" on the other. He does so by driving a wedge between the two orders in the introduction to the *Decameron*, ending his plague history with the most obtrusive of rhetorical devices.

> O quanti gran palagi, quante belle case, quanti nobili abituri, per adietro di famiglie pieni, di signori e di donne, infino al menomo fante rimaser voti! O quante memorabili schiatte, quante ampissime eredità, quante famose ricchezze si videro senza successor debito rimanere! Quanti valorosi uomini, quante belle donne, quanti leggiadri giovani, li quali non che altri, ma Galieno, Ipocrate, o Esculapio avrieno guidicati sanissimi, la mattina desinarono co' lor parenti, compagni, e amici, che poi la sera vegnente appresso nell'altro mondo cenaron con li lor passati! (16)[21]

Not only does the highly schematic structure of this passage call attention to Boccaccio's art, but the inclusion of the *ubi sunt* motif as well. His generous use of anaphora, with the repetition of the adjectives *quanti* and *quante*, reduces the list of nouns to a kind of paratactic sameness in which the emphasis falls on the modifiers rather than the substantives, with the result that our attention is drawn away from content and toward pure form.

This is not to suggest that Boccaccio's uneasy transition is the result of ineptitude, nor that it is an exercise in rhetoric for its own sake, but

[19] Ibid., p. 63.
[20] In "The Marginality of Literature," Mazzotta sees Boccaccio's entire enterprise as a meditation on this gap. See his p. 65.
[21] All quotations will be from Giovanni Boccaccio, *Decameron, edizione critica secondo l'autografo hamiltoniano*, ed. Vittora Branca (Florence: L'Accademia della Crusca, 1976). Page numbers will be included in the body of the text.

instead that it is a statement about the nature of his fictions and their relationship to history. By introducing his frame story with rhetoric, the writer is asserting its status as pure artifice, and the rhetorical ligature which connects the frame story with the preceding history betrays the radical discontinuity between these two narrative orders. The mediating passage thus serves less as a transition from history to fiction than as a commentary on their irreconcilability, and accordingly, the entire introduction to the *Decameron* may be read as a meditation on that schism.

A comparison between the plague chronicle and the frame story becomes, as we might expect, a study in antithesis. Out of the wreckage of disease-ridden Florence, Boccaccio creates a fiction of perfect order. Nothing could contrast more violently with the portrait of a dying city than this account of the pastoral beatitude enjoyed by the ten young people of the storytelling *brigata*.[22] Where decay and death tyrannize the city, youth and beauty grace this country outing. Where the social glue of the *polis* has come undone, ties of friendship, kinship, and love bind the *brigata*. Where horror and grief rule Florence, no bad news may penetrate the self-made walls of the pastoral retreat. Where decency and honor have fled the city, the *brigata* abounds in civic virtues.[23]

The polar opposition between history and fiction in the introduction needs no further proof. And with this, Boccaccio's first lesson in how to read the text is complete, for he has disabused the reader of any tendency to take his fictions at face value—as historically true in any way. Of course, the fact that the tales are not told directly by Boccaccio, but by a group of narrators who are themselves fictitious, places them at one more remove from the reader. Any temptation on our part to entertain the "referential fallacy" (by this I mean the assumption that the tales point to an extra-literary reality) is thus immediately thwarted by Boccaccio's insistence on dramatizing their telling. Not for a moment does he allow us to forget that the stories are fictional constructs—that they cannot be taken at face value—and implies instead the necessity of an allegorical reading in which surfaces give way to hidden truths.

But those truths will not inhere in any ideological pronouncements, nor in any moral *sovrasenso* which may be extracted from the content of the tales, for Boccaccio contradicts himself throughout the *Decame-*

[22] On the dichotomy city/country, sickness/health, see Francesco Tateo, "Il 'realismo' nella novella boccaccesca," in *Retorica e poetica fra medioevo e rinascimento* (Bari, 1960), p. 197, and Marga Cottino-Jones, "The City/Country Conflict in the *Decameron*," *Studi sul Boccaccio*, VIII (Florence, 1974), 152-157.

[23] Raffaello Ramat in *Saggi sul rinascimento* (Florence, 1969), p. 37, shows how the storytelling *brigata* is an exemplar for the ideal city.

ron, denying the relevance of absolute interpretive systems to his nar-rations. Indeed, no sooner is one ideological position articulated than its opposite appears to defy any reduction of the text to strict formula-tions of theme.[24] Walt Whitman could have been speaking for Boc-caccio when he said, "Do I contradict myself? / Very well then I con-tradict myself, / (I am large, I contain multitudes)." It is as if Dioneo, the most subversive of all the *brigata* in his refusal to adhere to the theme of the day, were included in the *Decameron* expressly to forbid the thematic critics any perfection of pattern, any interpretive key, any ideological complacency. But the failure of a strictly thematic reading is another clue to the readers that they must look elsewhere for the locus of meaning in this text.[25]

Of the critical positions outlined above, the Christian figural ap-proach and that of the history of ideas, I take the former as the most pernicious and therefore most worthy of redress, for it has given dignity to the long-standing bias against *Johannes tranquillitatum*. My task here will be to answer those who would accuse Boccaccio of an amoral exercise in aesthetics, and peripherally to suggest some weak-nesses in a strictly thematic approach, by showing how the writer manipulates his genre in polemic ways, using the *novella* form to interpret and evaluate its own content. Without directly positing a moral stance, Boccaccio embodies his teachings in the very mode of his narration, offering successful and unsuccessful examples of the storytelling art which will serve as models for the perspectives he would have us adopt as his reading public.[26] Although his art is a didactic one, that didacticism inheres not so much in direct moralizing content as in the subtle and ingenious ways in which he uses the mechanisms of the storytelling genre. The six chapters in this book

[24] Critics have often commented on the impossibility of finding in Boccaccio any ideological consistency. See Scaglione, p. 74; Natalino Sapegno, *Il Trecento* (Milan, 1934), p. 357; Thomas Greene, "Forms of Accommodation in the *Decameron*," *Italica*, 45 (1968), 297; Mario Baratto, *Realtà e stile nel 'Decameron'* (Vicenza, 1974), p. 87; and Carlo Salinari, "L'empirismo ideologico del Boccaccio," in *La critica della letteratura italiana* (Naples, 1973), p. 364.

[25] The structuralists, on the other hand, go too far in the direction of pure form to account for the uniqueness and irreducibility of the *Decameron*. For the classic applica-tion of Propp's findings to Boccaccio, see Tzvetan Todorov, *Grammaire du 'Décaméron'* (The Hague, 1969). For some of the numerous critics of Todorov's method, see Renato Barilli, "Semiologia e retorica nella lettura del *Decameron*," *Verri*, 35-36 (1970), 30-33; Nino Borsellino, "*Decameron* come teatro," in *Rozzi e intronati: Esperienze e forme di teatro dal 'Decameron' al 'Candelaio'* (Rome, 1976), p. 14; and Franco Fido, "Boccaccio's *Ars Narrandi* in the Sixth Day of the *Decameron*," in *Italian Literature: Roots and Branches, Essays in Honor of Thomas Goddard Bergin* (New Haven and London, 1976), pp. 226-227.

[26] Baratto sees in the *Decameron* the importance of a moral style which reflects, on an aesthetic level, the way in which man should confront his worldly experience. See his pp. 19 ff.

take as their subjects a sampling of tales, scattered throughout the
Decameron, representing various ways in which Boccaccio teaches us to
read the text. The stories I have selected contain important prescrip-
tions for their own interpretation, including such internalized artist
figures as Ser Ciappelletto and Fra Cipolla whose verbal constructs
alert us to the untrustworthiness of all human discourse. Internalized
publics bear witness to the forgeries of these two ecclesiastical impost-
ers and teach us, by their example, the dangers of too literal a belief in
both the written and the spoken word. In the Calandrino cycle of four
tales, the dupe gains center stage, and the tricksters fade into the
background[27] as Boccaccio makes his warning against reader gullibility ever more emphatic. The inclusion of a frame story of ten narrators who alternate as the listeners of each other's stories makes
explicit, on yet another textual level, the processes of telling and re-
ceiving tales. Although usually more sophisticated than the internalized publics of their stories, these ten youths are themselves prey to
a certain degree of naiveté when they occasionally miss the point of
their own narrations and thus warn us against automatically modeling
our responses on theirs. The very presence of this mediate public,
whose reactions to the tales become formal elements of the text, demands that we as readers consciously formulate our own response,
whether in agreement with that of the *brigata*, or in ironic contrast to
it.

Another way in which Boccaccio makes explicit the mechanics of
storytelling is by juxtaposing various narrative modes according to the
exigencies of the daily themes. Thus the second day's stories about the
primacy of fortune in human affairs belong to the romantic mode,
while the fourth day's stories about unhappy love are, of course,
tragic. If the *Decameron* may be read as Boccaccio's quest for an ideal
genre of narration to convey his meaning, then romance and tragedy
are detours in that quest, and comedy emerges as the mode most
congenial to Boccaccio's intent.

The *Decameron*, however, cannot be about the art of storytelling
without also being about the creation of a public capable of appreciat-
ing that art. In the final tale of the collection, Boccaccio subjects his
readers to the severest of tests, as Gualtieri himself tests the all-
suffering Griselda. With this story, which resists all univocal interpretations, the author challenges his public to entertain a multiplicity of
perspectives at once. It is in this refusal to give the text formal closure
that Boccaccio's allegory of form offers its most compelling lesson.
The absence of an ending which will perfect the work in the etymolog-

[27] See "Postilla critica a Calandrino e l'elitropia," in *Il Decameron*, ed. Luigi Russo
(Florence, 1939), p. 446.

ical sense, opens up the entire text to ambiguity, placing the burden of interpretation on the reader, who is by now well prepared to accept that responsibility.

I

PSEUDO-SAINTS AND STORYTELLERS

THE TALE OF SER CIAPPELLETTO (I, 1)[1]

Boccaccio's meticulous defense of his *Decameron* in the introduction to the fourth day and again in the conclusion to the text suggests his ongoing awareness of the threat he poses to the established traditions of medieval narrative. In answering his would-be critics, Boccaccio addresses himself to all but the most serious possible charges, using the long list of complaints as a foil for his area of greatest vulnerability. The detractors focus their attention on the content and style of the stories, sidetracking us from the remarkable changes which Boccaccio has worked on the genre itself. These formal innovations are much more subversive than any of the detractors' charges would suggest, for they challenge the very structure of medieval synthetic thought. Battaglia points out that prior to Boccaccio, prose narrative was used to exemplify eternal, fixed truths, thus affirming the operation of divine providence in human affairs.[2] Fictions were always pressed into the service of external dogma, and the narrative word was seen as a vehicle of the divine order it exemplified. But Boccaccio makes a radical break from this exemplary tradition, freeing his stories from any absolute interpretive systems, and clearing a new, non-dogmatic fictional space.[3] He does this by severing the conventional bonds be-

---

[1] This chapter is a revised version of an article entitled "Ser Ciappelletto: A Reader's Guide to the *Decameron*" published in *The Humanities Association Review*, 26 (Fall 1975), 275-288.

[2] See Battaglia, *Giovanni Boccaccio e la riforma della narrativa*, pp. 1-81.

[3] For his suggestive distinction between the medieval *exemplum*, with its deductive movement from the general to the specific, and Boccaccio's "exemplary" mode, where "una norma ideale" is extracted from concrete experience in an inductive movement from the specific to the general (within the human order), see Tateo, "Il 'realismo' della novella boccaccesca," pp. 198-200.

tween concrete experience and transcendent truth implicit in the *exemplum*, forcing his readers to examine the expectations they bring to the text, and to revise them in the light of dissonant and jarring narrations. The author must disabuse his public of the tendency to interpret stories in exemplary terms by making the *exemplum* discredit itself. In his threshold story, Boccaccio reveals the utter inadequacy of this traditional approach to explain the outrageous saga of the sinner who bluffs his way into sainthood, thereby exposing the obsolescence of the genre he so successfully transforms, and setting forth the ground rules for a new and startling narrative mode.

Panfilo prefaces the story of Ser Ciappelletto with a divine invocation and a long theoretical commentary on the meaning of the tale.[4] "Convenevole cosa è, carissime donne, che ciascheduna cosa la quale l'uomo fa, dallo ammirabile e santo nome di Colui, il quale di tutte fu facitore, le dea principio" (26). This opening statement appears to be nothing more than a standard rhetorical device, as Panfilo acknowledges literary decorum with the formulaic "convenevole cosa è," and obliges by beginning the work in the name of the divine principle which orders the universe. The invocation could stop here, but the narrator prolongs it by making God the author of the tale he is about to tell. Though this may appear to be a conventional claim for narrative authenticity, Panfilo's insistence on the subtleties of divine motivation go beyond the dictates of decorum. "Per che, dovendo io al vostro novellare, sì come primo, dare cominciamento, intendo da una delle sue maravigliose cose incominciare" (26). This will be a miracle tale, with an explicit didactic intent, "acciò che, quella udita, la nostra speranza in Lui, sì come in cosa impermutabile, si fermi e sempre sia da noi il suo nome lodato" (26). The tale promises to bear witness to God's providential design, and to inspire faith in its workings. Panfilo follows this exhortation with a discourse on the function of saints as mediators between the chaotic world of men and the inaccessible reaches of the divine. His rhetorical tone continues as he introduces the second discussion with "manifesta cosa è," echoing the "convenevole cosa è" formula of the invocation. The prose is thick with repetitions and elaborations which correspond to the chaos of the human condition as he describes it.[5]

---

[4] Alfredo Schiaffini sees in this preamble a stilted virtuosity which is in marked contrast to the fluid and relaxed quality of much of Boccaccio's prose style, as exemplified by the deathbed exchange between Ser Ciappelletto and the friar confessor later on in the tale. See *Tradizione e poesia nella prosa d'arte italiana dalla latinità medievale a Giovanni Boccaccio* (Genova, 1934), p. 279.

[5] In *Boccaccio medievale* (Florence, 1970), p. 51, Vittore Branca cites this passage to exemplify the rhetorical devices used by Boccaccio throughout the *Decameron* to create complexity and ambiguity.

Manifesta cosa è che, sì come le cose temporali tutte sono transitorie e mortali, così in sé e fuor di sé esser piene di noia, d'angoscia e di fatica e a infiniti pericoli sogiacere; alle quali senza niuno fallo né potremmo noi, che viviamo mescolati in esse e che siamo parte d'esse, durare né ripararci, se spezial grazia di Dio forza e avvedimento non ci prestasse. (26)

The dense, repetitive style of this passage reinforces the contrast between human disorder and divine grace which will be its salvation. Each descriptive is paired or tripled with synonyms. The temporal order is described by three equivalent adjectives: "le cose temporali tutte sono transitorie e mortali." The construction "così in sé e fuor di sé" is echoed soon after by "viviamo mescolati in esse e che siamo parte d'esse." "Di noia, d'angoscia, e di fatica" is another triad, with "infiniti pericoli" tacked on as a seeming afterthought. "Durare né ripararci" constitutes a final synonymous pair. The only element of this passage which escapes redundancy is the qualifier: "se spezial grazia di Dio forza e avvedimento non ci prestasse." It is appropriate that the dense language describing human chaos would find its relief in this promise of divine redemption.

After presenting the radical gap between the sublunar world and the realm of God, the narrator suggests that this distance is bridged by certain privileged beings. Those who have once been human, but are now among the blessed in heaven, would be the ideal conveyors of human prayer. So far, the doctrine is conventional and unsurprising. Perhaps only the word *procuratore*[6] may strike us as slightly out of place, for it implies a body of extraneous, commercial associations which may distract us from the teaching at hand. Panfilo proceeds to explain that man in his blindness may sanctify someone truly worthy of damnation; but he assures us that God will not be prejudiced against those prayers which are addressed to a false saint, provided that the motives of the suppliant are pure.

Panfilo maintains the measured tone of this discourse, as if nothing remarkable were being said here. But the notion of a canonized sinner, and of God's indifference to the quality of his saints, is both shocking in itself and contradicts the thrust of his previous argument. Until now the narrator has insisted on the vast gap between God and man, bridgeable only by saints. But in the case of the false saint, where God will ignore the intercessor in favor of the suppliant, it seems that prayers arrive at their divine destination unmediated. Why, then, have intercessors at all?

---

[6] "Procuratore: chi cura, amministra i beni altrui con mandato del padrone." Carlo Battisti, Giovanni Alessio, *Dizionario etimologico italiano*, IV (Florence, 1954), 3091.

The teller ends his introduction with the promise that his tale will make manifest his teaching ("il che manifestamente portrà apparire nella novella la quale di raccontare intendo: manifestamente, dico, non il giudicio di Dio ma quel degli uomini seguitando") (27). This last assertion echoes the beginning "manifesta cosa è" of his preamble, making it appear to be a perfectly symmetrical statement of didactic intent. Yet Panfilo's point is anything but *manifesta*. The narrator makes his teaching hopelessly ambiguous by adding "manifestamente, dico, non il giudicio di Dio ma quel degli uomini seguitando." Panfilo completely undercuts his discourse by suggesting that all he has said represents the limited point of view of mankind which he has previously characterized as so precarious and flawed that the reader will have difficulty assigning it any authority at all. Furthermore, in describing the chaos of the human order, Panfilo has included himself in this constituency by the use of the first person plural in "viviamo mescolati in esse." Though he holds out the possibility of another perspective from which man may view the human condition—the perspective offered by divine grace—he later rejects that possibility by saying that he speaks from the very untranscendent perspective of man, with no pretensions to a vantage point *sub specie aeternitatis*. Thus, even though he is a spokesman for a theological truth and a human example of it, Panfilo claims no privileged position from which to argue. And it is here that Boccaccio's novelty resides—in his bold abandonment of narrative authority. To admit the precariousness of the human condition is commonplace, but to admit the contingency of the authorial voice which comments on that condition is a striking and courageous innovation.

What Boccaccio is trying to do in the introduction to the tale, then, is to underscore the difficulties implicit in the statement "manifesta cosa è." The arrogance of any pretension to incarnate divine providence in literature is really the subject of this story. Thus, the very confusion with which Panfilo makes his promise to tell a tale of providential significance undermines both his claim and the entire moralizing commentary which accompanies it. By announcing a miracle tale ("intendo da una delle sue maravigliose cose incominciare"), by offering an inconsistent theological teaching, by promising to show *manifestamente* this doctrine according to the judgment of man, which he has previously characterized as hopelessly immersed in error, Panfilo abdicates any possibility of a serious didactic intent. Yet the story bespeaks its own truth—one which baffles the narrator's attempts at explication.[7] A close reading of this text will reveal the lesson it teaches, and the inappropriateness of Panfilo's exegesis.

[7] In *Forma e ideologia* (Naples, 1974), p. 36, Giancarlo Mazzacurati sees an outright contradiction between the tale of Ser Ciappelletto and the obsolete religious orthodoxy of its preamble.

Ser Ciappelletto, an unscrupulous notary from Prato is commissioned by a rich merchant of France, Musciatto Franzesi, to oversee some business matters in the provinces. The notary transfers himself to Burgundy where he is received into the home of two Florentine usurers. During his stay, Ciappelletto becomes mortally ill and decides to spare his hosts the embarrassment of dying unredeemed in their home. He summons a local friar and produces a confessional self-portrait of such extravagant virtue that the friar takes him for a holy man. On the eve of Ciappelletto's burial, the friar brings the case before his parishioners who eagerly welcome their newest saint.

The tale is a perfectly realized example of a false self-transformation in which the protagonist's sins catalogued at the beginning are mirrored and reversed by his "virtues" as they are listed by the friar at the conclusion of the story.[8] The transformation is prefigured by the change in his name from Cepparello, meaning "small log," with its connotations of phallic insignificance, to Ciappelletto, which Boccaccio tells us means "little garland," with its associations of beauty and grace. "Non sappiendo li franceschi che si volesse dir Cepparello, credendo che 'cappello,' cioè 'ghirlanda' secondo il lor volgare a dir venisse, per ciò che piccolo era come dicemmo, non Ciappello ma Ciappelletto il chiamavano" (27). But this transformation is a false one, and serves as a miniature of the final transformation to sainthood, which is based on similarly false premises. Here it is appropriate to make explicit what Boccaccio does not—that the most suggestive French equivalent of Ciappelletto is *chapelet*, or "rosary."[9] This linguistic misunderstanding anticipates the climactic misunderstanding of the parishioners who will erroneously sanctify Ciappelletto. The verbal distortions of the name suggest the nature of Ciappelletto's ultimate distortion, for it too is linguistic. He has created in words a false self and that linguistic creation is canonized.

The mistranslation of Ciappelletto's name points to something in the nature of the public which invites its final deception. The French assume that their language gives a correct equivalent of Cep-

[8] Giovanni Getto suggests that the whole story works on the dynamic of reversal. Describing the radical contrast between Ciappelletto's physical inconsequentiality and his moral enormity in *Vita di forme e forme di vita nel 'Decameron'* (Turin, 1958), p. 46, Getto sees the principle of reversal at work. Guido Almansi is also alert to this principle, finding in it the medieval motif of *adynaton*. See *The Writer as Liar*, pp. 28 and 36. Marga Cottino-Jones sees a linguistic-stylistic equivalent to this opposition in the alternative uses of augmentative and diminuitive tones throughout the *novella*. For an analysis of these linguistic motifs, see her chapter "Ser Ciappelletto or 'Le Saint Noir': A Comic Paradox" in *An Anatomy of Boccaccio's Style* (Naples, 1968), pp. 23-51.

[9] That the rosary was extant in Boccaccio's time is suggested by scholarly speculation on the origin of this rite. Its source has been traced back to two centuries before Boccaccio. See the *New Catholic Encyclopedia* (New York, 1967), p. 668. I am indebted to my colleague Richard Grant for suggesting the possibility of this interpretation.

parello, though in truth it offers only an approximation, and hence a body of misleading associations. Their readiness to understand everything in their own terms, never doubting the appropriateness of those terms, opens them to Ciappelletto's final verbal manipulations. The friar too believes in the inviolability of his own language—that of confession and absolution—for it is unquestioningly used to determine the saintly credentials of Ser Ciappelletto. When the gullible friar hears the coherent and persuasive confession of the dying man, he has no doubt that his measure of holiness has found him a saint.

The all-pervasive theme of credulity comes under special attack in this tale. In the guise of *fede*, gullibility wins the day, as faith appears in a multitude of equivocal contexts throughout the story. Musciatto Franzesi, in search of an agent to manage his affairs while he is a-broad, seeks someone whose depravity is equal to that of his clients. He racks his brains "e a lui non andava per la memoria chi tanto malvagio uom fosse, in cui egli potesse alcuna fidanza avere, che opporre alla loro malvagità si potesse" (27). *Fidanza* here occurs in a rather unexpected context; though the notion of trust ultimately conjures up expectations of human goodness, here Musciatto's hopes are of wickedness and an absence of any moral compunction. The use of *fidanza* in a context which denies the usual implications of the word is a technique which Boccaccio has used before. When discussing sainthood in terms of *procuratori* he introduced a whole body of worldly, bureaucratic associations. These reversals of our expectations put us on guard and make us question our stock responses to language. Panfilo's use of the word *procuratori* quietly raised our suspicions about his teachings on sainthood. In the same way, the mention of *fidanza* in a context which nullifies our conventional expectations makes us question our readiness to believe.

The theme of breaking faith is the very key to Ser Ciappelletto's character. It is the first thing we learn about him, as it is indeed his greatest pleasure in life. "Egli, essendo notaio, avea grandissima vergogna quando uno de' suoi strumenti, come che pochi ne facesse, fosse altro che falso trovato" (27). Here again Boccaccio uses a word in a context which totally negates our expectations of language. Ciappelletto experiences "grandissima vergogna," implying some tender moral sensibility, when his documents are found out to be anything but false. The syntax of the period, which allows the greatest possible distance between *vergogna* and the reason for it, prolongs our expectations and makes their denial that much more striking.[10]

---

[10] Almansi points out Boccaccio's use of antiphrasis continually to thwart our expectations of language. See his p. 36.

So great is his joy in making false documents that "tanti avrebbe fatti di quanti fosse stato richesto, e quegli più volentieri in dono che alcuno altro grandemente salariato" (27). The extravagance of these statements corresponds to the extravagant way in which Ser Ciappelletto will ultimately use his flair for falsification. Just as his description begins with *testimonianze false*, so his life will end with *testimonianze false*. The only difference will be that his initial forgeries were secular, and his final ones are spiritual. His last *testimonianza falsa* thus becomes the appropriate fulfillment of a life whose theme was the inspiration of false trust.[11] "Testimonianze false con sommo diletto diceva, richesto e non richesto; e dandosi a quei tempi in Francia a' saramenti grandissima fede, non curandosi fargli falsi, tante quistioni malvagiamente vincea a quante a giurare di dire il vero sopra la sua fede era chiamato" (27-28). The theme of faith is here significantly revised. Appearing twice in one period, its meaning oscillates from credulity ("dandosi a quei tempi in Francia a' saramenti grandissima fede") to false pledges of sincerity ("a giurare di dire il vero sopra la sua fede era chiamato"). The term recurs climactically at the end of the tale, where it assumes its final, decisive meaning: gullibility. The parishioners listen to the friar with "intera fede" (36) as they flock to worship their most recent saint.

With the canonization of the sinner, the transformation of Ser Cepparello to San Ciappelletto is complete. Boccaccio has given us a witty and well-turned narrative, satisfying in its own terms and brilliantly parodying stock medieval forms. But the question remains: why did the author choose this particular tale to initiate his *Decameron*? Panfilo's conclusion to the tale suggests some possible answers. "E se così è, grandissima si può la benignità di Dio cognoscere verso noi, la quale non al nostro errore ma alla purità della fé riguardando, così faccendo noi nostro mezzano un suo nemico, amico credendolo, ci essaudisce, come se a uno veramente santo per mezzano della sua grazia ricorressimo" (37). The pious tone of this lesson only thinly veils its sacrilegious import. If Panfilo's explanation holds, then God has duped the faithful by disguising a sinner as a saint, employing the same tactics as Ciappelletto himself to facilitate his ends. Where the notary used words to deceive, God uses the man himself as his vehicle of deception, making Ser Ciappelletto a grotesque parody of the Logos—the lie made flesh.

Is Panfilo aware of the blasphemous implications of his commentary, or is he too among the divinely duped? This question suggests a major interpretive problem in the *Decameron*: to what extent is Boc-

---

[11] In "The Marginality of Literature," p. 70, Mazzotta points out this ironic consistency in Ciappelletto's career.

caccio speaking through his ten storytellers? Does he pose an ironic distance between himself and his interlocutors, and if so, what is the nature of that disparity? In the case of the first story, such a determination must rest on an analysis of Panfilo's tone in offering his exegesis. If he is indeed serious, then we must conclude that the narrator is not aware of the meaning of his tale, and that Boccaccio is smiling at his simplicity. But if Panfilo is himself smiling as he offers his pious remarks, then we need not posit an ironic distance between the storyteller and Boccaccio himself.

One index to the narrator's tone is the response of the listeners to the tale and to its moral package. "La novella di Panfilo fu in parte risa e tutta commendata dalle donne" (38). The reaction of the women suggests that the story was received as a humorous example ("in parte risa") of a solemn truth ("tutta commendata"). The impact of the lesson is verified by its recurrence as the theme of the subsequent story. "Mostrato n'ha Panfilo nel suo novellare la benignità di Dio non guardare a' nostri errori, quando da cosa che per noi veder non si possa procedano" (38). It seems, then, that the listeners have taken Panfilo's moralizing commentary at face value. Their general acceptance of his conclusion and Neifile's pursuance of it in her own story seem to indicate universal agreement with the lesson that he draws from his tale.

Yet we have seen how Panfilo's well-intentioned effort to credit God with the events of the story turns into a blasphemous indictment of divine means. God becomes nothing more than a transcendent version of the very sinner he masquerades as a saint. Here, let us back up for a moment and reassert the distinction between narrator and author, lest Boccaccio himself be credited with the irreverence to which Panfilo unwittingly gives words. In showing us the grotesque extremes of Panfilo's thought, the writer is not himself blaspheming God, but exposing the blasphemous direction of such logic. The assumption that man can discern God's will as it manifests itself in human events is arrogant and misguided, and Boccaccio is attacking this approach especially as a basis for narrative. If man cannot decipher divine motives in ordering events, how can he possibly exemplify transcendent truths in his stories?

By taking an example of what appears to be God's malice toward man, and by twisting that into greater proof of his benevolence, Boccaccio suggests the folly of any human attempt to understand and render divine meaning in *exempla*.[12] So adamant is he in his belief that

---

[12] On the other hand, critics who take Panfilo at his word and read this as a tale which truly illustrates divine providence at work include Giorgio Padoan in "Mondo aristocratico e mondo communale," p.164, and T.K. Seung in *Cultural Thematics: The Formation of the Faustian Ethos* (New Haven, 1976), pp. 194-201.

it recurs as the theme of the following tale in which Abraam Giudeo (I, 2) finds the squalor of the Vatican paradoxical proof of God's love of the Church.

As storyteller and moralizer of his own tale, Panfilo stands midway between two diametrically opposed publics: the deceived parish within the story, and the demystified reading public. The narrator knows the lie of Ciappelletto's sainthood, yet he insists on seeing that forgery as proof of divine benevolence. Though Panfilo is aware of one level of deception, he is still the dupe of a kind of logic which insists on reading divine motivation into all human events. We the reading public are privy to the folly of the teller's logic, for we see the absurd extremes to which he is led as he makes God into a super-Ciappelletto. Thus Panfilo and the parishoners suffer from similar, though varying degrees of, the same bias. The narrator's claim to speak providential truths is as naive in its way as the parishioners' simple belief in Ciappelletto's sanctity. Both views share the premise that God's will is humanly intelligible, though they differ in how man may ultimately express his understanding of divine truths. The deceived Burgundians believe in the machinery of the Church as the purveyor of God's will on earth, holding that an institution must mediate between the believers and the final object of their belief. The existence of saints is an extension of the need for intermediaries between man and God, so that their function becomes analogous to the Church itself. The insistence that man must address God through an institution is carried one step further by the notion of a saintly middleman.

Accordingly, Panfilo's moral commentary on his tale can be taken in an anticlerical sense.[13] If God will bypass the saint in favor of the suppliant, why bother with mediators at all? This attack on the doctrine of saintly intercession is implicit throughout the story.[14] Setting

---

[13] The proto-Lutheran implications of this tale may not be lost on the modern reader, as they obviously were not lost on earlier ones whose anticlerical biases found kindred attitudes in the tales of Ser Ciappelletto and Abraam Giudeo. According to Jules Bonnet, Olympia Morata was such a reader of these tales when she translated them into Latin for the court of Ferrara in the mid-sixteenth century. Bonnet sees signs of Morata's own burgeoning Protestantism in her desire to translate particularly these tales. See Jules Bonnet, *Vie d'Olympia Morata: Épisode de la renaissance et de la réforme en Italie* (Paris, 1850), pp. 51-52. On the anticlerical uses of the *Decameron*, see Hauvette, *Boccace: Étude biographique et littéraire*, p. 281, and Neri, "Il disegno ideale del *Decameron*," p. 54, who both mention the striking example of Olympia Morata. Mario Baratto, in *Realtà e stile nel 'Decameron'*, p. 207, discusses the growing schism between Christianity as belief and as institution—a break to which Boccaccio bears witness.

[14] Several critics read this tale as a critique of the doctrine of saintly mediation. See V. Šklovsky, *Lettura del 'Decameron': Dal romanzo d'avventura al romanzo di carattere*, trans. Alessandro Ivanov (Bologna, 1969), pp. 205-206; and Arturo Graf, *Miti, leggende, e superstitizioni del medio evo* (Turin, 1925), p. 368. The element of superstition which Marga Cottino-Jones points out in the cult of Ser Ciappelletto constitutes a further

aside the question of Ser Ciappelletto's qualifications for the position, sainthood seems to play to the lowest possible religious motives.[15] The friar wants a saint buried in his church so that it can be the site of miracles, thus increasing the attendance at his services, while the believers are hungry for relics and personal favors obtained through the intercession of the saint. By praying to this kind of mediator, the congregation is not addressing the God of Moses and Christ, but the god of self-aggrandizement and material gain. That prayer which stops short of God, which rests on a middleman who, one hopes, will put in a good word at the top, is thinly disguised idolatry. Ser Ciappelletto is the ideal recipient of such passions, for his life represents the self-seeking materialism of his constituency.

Insofar as Panfilo's commentary is anticlerical, he remains true to the tale he tells. But he fails to consider a deeper, more threatening moral problem posed by the false saint. Ser Ciappelletto is a storyteller whose tale inspires faith, pretending to be an expression of God's will manifest in human life. In the same way, Panfilo is a storyteller who claims to figure divine truths in his tale *manifestamente*. It seems that literature here runs the risk of functioning as the false saint. Panfilo's promise to be the conveyor of divine truths makes literature a middleman, a palpable extension of the Word, in order to render it accessible to human understanding. Indeed, both saints and literature occupy a middling position between the divine and the human. The danger of a literature which attempts to mediate between these realms is that it may misrepresent the divine, become an object of worship in itself, and evoke the worst kind of faith in its readers. Panfilo does not see this danger in making providential claims for his tale, but Boccaccio does see the problem, and seeks to demystify his readers by identifying his work with the false saint.

In his final attempt to make God responsible for the sanctification of this sinner, Panfilo calls Ciappelletto *mezzano*. Perhaps our initial inclination would be to suppress the scabrous connotations of this term—indeed, Panfilo would want us to do so. But Boccaccio asks us to retain the equivocal meaning and to consider the analogy between pandering and literature. If this quintessential storyteller, Ser Ciappelletto, is a *mezzano*, so indeed is the *Decameron* itself, which Boccaccio subtitled *Prencipe Galeotto*, recalling Gallehaut, the mediator between

---

criticism of the concept of saintly intercession. See her "Magic and Superstition in Boccaccio's *Decameron*," in *Italian Quarterly*, 18 (Spring 1975), 8-9.

[15] Saint worship is promoted by the increasingly fragmented, material nature of religious faith in the Middle Ages. J. Huizinga comments on the danger implicit in the proliferation of saintly icons in *The Waning of the Middle Ages*, trans. F. Hopman (Garden City, 1954), pp. 165-177.

Lancelot and Guinevere in the Arthurian legend.[16] By associating his book with the archetypal panderer of medieval romance, Boccaccio imitates Dante's device to expose the seductions of literature. Francesca calls the book *Galeotto* (*Inf.*, V, 137) as she describes the catalytic function of the text in her affair with Paolo. It was *la lettura* which made explicit the adulterous desires of the lovers and sanctioned their liaison. "Galeotto fu il libro e chi lo scrisse"[17] laments Francesca as she confesses her sin, while idealizing it in the name of her Arthurian models.

The passage in *Inferno* V is an excellent gloss on Boccaccio's subtitle to his *Decameron*. While Francesca identifies the book with the procurer of illicit favors, Boccaccio does her one better. Not only is his book a Prencipe Galeotto, pandering to the erotic desires of the reading public, it is also an analogue to the false saint, playing to their counterfeit spiritual needs. Yet saintly mediation here poses a danger which erotic mediation does not. For the saintly middleman not only procures favors for his suppliants, but also threatens to replace the divine as an object of worship. Where Galeotto remains middleman between the suitor and the object of desire, the saint becomes the object of desire in an idolatrous substitution of means for ends.

The first tale, in all its richness and complexity, serves as a solemn warning to readers of the *Decameron*. This work is not to be read as any manifestation of a divine order, nor will it serve as a false mediator between human understanding and eternal truths. Boccaccio seeks to free his work from any absolute interpretive systems, demanding that the stories be read and received on their own terms, without recourse to extranarrative ideologies. The tale of Ser Ciappelletto, however, is not simply a negative example of how to read the *Decameron*, for it also suggests ways in which we might positively construe the text. The various publics represented in the first tale organize themselves in concentric circles, beginning with the innermost public of the deceived parish, moving out to the encircling public of the *brigata*,[18] and then to the all-enclosing public of the general read-

[16] Mazzotta discusses the great literary reverberations of this allusion, and suggests Boccaccio's self-deprecatory intent in affixing this subtitle to his work in "The Marginality of Literature," pp. 68-69. Joy Hambuechen Potter discusses the semiotic implications of this subtitle, or "nickname," in a manuscript in preparation at the time of this writing. For a history of the debate surrounding the subtitle, see Robert Hollander, *Boccaccio's Two Venuses* (New York, 1977), pp. 102-105.

[17] All quotes from the works of Dante come from Dante Alighieri, *Tutte le opere*, ed. Fredi Chiappelli (Milan, 1969).

[18] The suggestive reading of Nino Borsellino in "*Decameron* come teatro" has led Antonio Stäuble to look closely at the frame story youths as the audience of narrative spectacle in his essay "La brigata del *Decameron* come pubblico teatrale," in *Studi sul Boccaccio*, IX (Florence, 1975-1976), 103-117.

ership. The concentric circles represent varying degrees of gullibility, ranging from the absolute credulousness of the parishioners to the more sophisticated, though still mystified *brigata*, which insists on reading divine motivation into human events. Implicit in this continuous chain of gullibilities, though ever more dilute as the public enlarges its perspective and becomes aware of the limitations of the encircled communities, is that there is no absolutely correct interpretation possible within the human order. Boccaccio's multiplication of gullible publics implies an infinite regression of such publics, each a little less credulous than the last, for human interpretation will always be subject to false appearances and deliberate deceptions. Thus we, the readers, must not fall prey to the illusions of the two enclosed publics.[19] We must not believe that our interpretation of the narrative is in any sense final, and always allow for alternative, less obvious explanations of literary events.

There is an analogue to the demystified perspective of this outermost public within the tale itself. The two Florentine brothers, Ciappelletto's hosts, occupy a privileged position as audience of the dying man's confession. They are seated in an adjoining room, listening through the wall with all the knowledge of the vast disparity between Ser Ciappelletto's fabrications and the truth of his life. Their comments are illuminating. "Che uomo è costui, il quale né vecchiezza né infermità né paura di morte, alla qual si vede vicino, né ancora di Dio, dinanzi al giudicio del quale di qui a picciola ora s'aspetta di dovere essere, dalla sua malvagità l'hanno potuto rimuovere, né far che egli così non voglia morire come egli è vivuto?" (35). Privy to the truth of Ciappelletto's life, and the enormity of his lies, the two brothers can do nothing but marvel at his death-defying ability to tell a story without any fear of the consequences. They represent a kind of totally demystified public, freed from illusions about the ethical or historical pretensions of storytelling.

Ironically, Ciappelletto's final act of generosity assures him eternal damnation within the Christian framework. Yet his gesture promises a kind of salvation for his hosts. Not only will they be saved from the embarrassment of harboring a dead, unredeemed guest, but also they will be saved from the foolish illusions of the parishoners who believe in Ciappelletto's sanctity. The privileged position of the two brothers is similar to our position as the knowing public.[20] Thus the

---

[19] These inner publics may be seen as examples of the "fictive readers" described by Lowry Nelson, Jr., in "The Fictive Reader and Literary Self-Reflexiveness," *The Disciplines of Criticism*, ed. Peter Demetz, Thomas Greene, and Lowry Nelson, Jr. (New Haven, 1968), pp. 173-191.

[20] Mazzotta identifies the two eavesdropping brothers with the reading public. See "The Marginality of Literature," p. 75.

anomalous quality of Ciappelletto's kindness to his hosts, after a lifetime of iniquity, may be explained in terms of his role as storyteller. No matter how unscrupulous the notary is to his gullible victims, he still feels a responsibility toward his hosts as the knowledgeable, demystified audience of his confession. Indeed, Ser Ciappelletto's damnation may be seen as the salvation of his reading public.

*

*   *

The opening tale of the *Decameron* is an extensive meditation on the ethics of storytelling. And what makes the moral question so compelling is the power to influence publics which this narrative suggests. Ciappelletto's fictive confession becomes the basis of a cult and reveals the nature of its constituents through the common bond which it elicits. Guiseppe Mazzotta points out the paradox of Ciappelletto's role as posthumous community organizer. "The self-loving man who was alien to the world and who lived in profanation of the world is sanctified and becomes, through his verbal disguise, the center of cohesion and stability of the community of man."[21] Ser Ciappelletto's false confession is an example *in malo* of how storytelling creates communities. But Boccaccio reverses that process. He creates a community by exposing Ciappelletto's deception. Boccaccio's public will thus be bound by a common mistrust of narrative and by a desire to go beyond the fiction in search of possible concealed meanings.

It is curious that Boccaccio would open his collection with such a devastating statement about fiction. Ciappelletto's narrative distortion suggests that stories can never be taken seriously on a purely literal level. Yet the tale gives us more than just the record of Ciappelletto's lie. It also provides enough information about his character and motivation for us to judge his fiction. Narrative thus serves to undercut its own mechanism, being most truthful when it calls itself into question. The tale of Ser Ciappelletto suggests both the deceptive quality of fictive creation and the power of fiction to expose its deception.

In his interpretation of this tale, Guido Almansi suggests that we interpret Ser Ciappelletto as the storyteller *par excellence*—hence his book's title, *The Writer as Liar*. But Ser Ciappelletto's lie is circumscribed by several layers of fictions which explain it and expose it *as* a lie. The narrative context of Ser Ciappelletto's forgery betrays its primary falsehood, while the frame story surrounding the tale reveals a subtler fallacy: the assumption of divine authority for human utterance. By overlaying Ser Ciappelletto's lie with two coatings of explanatory fictions, Boccaccio makes literature the agent of its own

[21] Ibid., p. 70.

exposure. If the writer is a liar, as Almansi suggests, then he is his own worst stool-pigeon—a teller of tales and of tattletales whose ironic counterpoint creates a continuous, vigilant commentary on the storytelling process.

The seriousness of Boccaccio's attempt to demystify his readers and honestly to define his narrative limits has been woefully misunderstood by his critics. The author's refusal to make providential claims for his work has been consistently confused with frivolity and escapism—confusion which has resulted in a grave misreading of this author's intentions. In the tale of Ser Ciappelletto, and indeed throughout the entire *Decameron*, Boccaccio reveals a serious preoccupation with questions of faith, honesty, and the status of human artifacts in the divine order.

Unlike Dante, whose ethical concerns are the explicit subject of his works, Boccaccio has no moralizing content. This unwillingness personally to enter and judge his material has been mistaken for indifference by many critics. What they fail to recognize is that Boccaccio's stories are self-judging, that as the teller generates his public through the act of storytelling, the nature of the emergent community reveals the morality of the tale. Boccaccio need only show us the quality of the public summoned by the story for us to judge the moral consequences of a given narrative. Ciappelletto's fictive confession produced a community bound by ignorance and self-interest. Later, Melchisedech's story of the three rings (I, 3) will create in Saladino a friendly, trustful storytelling public.[22] Boccaccio thus uses this built-in mechanism, the public dimension, to reveal and interpret the morality of his tales. The dynamics of storytelling allow him to comment on his narrative without compromising the objectivity of his voice.

It is in his flagrant misreading of the tale of Ser Ciappelletto that Auerbach betrays the weakness of his Christian figural approach to Boccaccio. This interpretation of a text in terms of its relation to biblical typology is valid for works whose literal level yields a complete and coherent moral reading. But in a work whose content cannot be understood apart from its form, whose literal level is not morally intelligible without a consideration of genre, Auerbach's interpretation falls short. Boccaccio's morality eludes a mere analysis of content, for the genre demands a study of the public consequences of storytelling.[23] Instead, Auerbach's approach to Ser Ciappelletto leads him to

[22] For a more complete study of the rhetorical powers of storytelling as revealed in this tale, see my article "Faith's Fiction: A Gloss on the Tale of Melchisedech and the Three Rings (I, 3)," to appear in *Canadian Journal of Italian Studies*.

[23] Azzurra B. Givens remarks on the importance of internal publics throughout the *Decameron* in *La dottrina d'amore nel Boccaccio* (Florence, 1968), pp. 184, 190.

the following conclusion: "there is no doubt, Boccaccio reports the monstrous adventure only for the sake of the comic effect of the two scenes mentioned above [the confession and sanctification of Ser Ciappelletto], and avoids any serious evaluation or taking of position."[24] Thus, what the critic takes for moral indifference on Boccaccio's part is what really makes this tale such a powerful, complicated statement on the ethics of storytelling. Boccaccio's refusal to inveigh against his protagonist reveals the profound, very Christian humility of a writer who makes no pretense to absolute authority. To berate Ser Ciappelletto would be to assume a kind of moral superiority for his own perspective, and Boccaccio would never hazard such a claim. The story of Ser Ciappelletto's false confession may be seen as profoundly Christian when read as a commentary on the limits of human narrative, and its inability to incarnate divine truths. As a warning to the reader not to be seduced into a form of idol worship by placing absolute faith in the human word, Boccaccio's metaliterary statement falls into a time-honored Christian tradition.

The opening story of the *Decameron* is thus a revelation of the possibilities of narrative within the human order. Though man's stories can never incarnate divine truths, they do have the power to create and determine their publics. This power can be grievously exploited, as in the case of Ser Ciappelletto, or it can be positively employed to refine and enlighten a community. But before fiction can be pressed into the service of didactic intent, its status as artifact must be made clear. Storytellers with pretensions to providential understanding will function as false saints, masquerading as mediators between man and God. In order to escape this danger, human fiction must expose its status as nontruth. Once this has been established, narrative can go on to reveal its teachings.

With this cautious, unassuming approach to his art, Boccaccio has moved a vast distance from the exemplary mode of his predecessors. Whereas the *exemplum* poses as literal truth, continuous with the divine order it manifests, Boccaccio warns us not to take narrative as an absolute article of faith to be imitated or rejected by the reader in defiance of the distinction between fiction and fact. In the disillusioning tale of Ser Ciappelletto, Boccaccio dramatizes the often flawed, morally suspect quality of human discourse, and discourages our indiscriminant acceptance of narrative authority—including, of course, his own.[25] He challenges the public to revise its reading habits, to abandon its didactic expectations, and to come to the text freed from

[24] See Auerbach, *Mimesis*, p. 230.
[25] On the metaliterary significance of this tale, see Mazzotta, "The Marginality of Literature," p. 69.

the biases of the exemplary tradition. Ser Ciappelletto waits at the threshold of the *Decameron*, bidding us set aside the preconceptions of the storytelling past, and to enter fresh into the rich and surprising world of the tales.

II

SPINNING THE WHEEL OF FORTUNE

THE TALES OF ANDREUCCIO (II, 5), BERITOLA (II, 6)
AND ALATIEL (II, 7)

Although the stories of Day I take place in a world whose Church, monarchy, and feudal code are found wanting, Boccaccio offers hope for improvement in the reformatory wit of his protagonists. Thus, delinquent monarchs are shaken into an awareness of their irresponsibility by the clever expedients of Melchisedech (I, 3), the lady of Gascony (I, 9), and the marchioness of Monferrato (I, 5). The Church is the target of witty reproach by the fallen monk of I, 4 and the friar inquisitor of I, 6, while two negligent practitioners of the feudal code, Can Grande della Scala (I, 7) and Erminio de' Grimaldi (I, 8), are brought back into line by the remarks of glib courtiers. Day I may be seen as a sustained lesson in the power of wit to reform delinquent authorities who would not tolerate direct criticism from their subordinates.[1] Boccaccio illustrates the lightning-fast consequences of such a strategy on the miserly Erminio de' Grimaldi: "così subitamente il prese una vergogna tale, che ella ebbe forza di fargli mutare animo quasi tutto in contrario" (62), while the recalcitrant Can Grande della Scala is immediately brought around by the veiled reproach of Bergamino: "Messer Cane, il quale intendente signore era, senza altra dimostrazione alcuna ottimamente intese ciò che dir volea Bergamino" (58). So effective is this method that it is said to 'awaken' the derelict authority, as in the case of the king of Cyprus who is forced out of his royal lethargy: "quasi dal sonno si risvegliasse" (64).

It is significant that Boccaccio begins his *Decameron* with examples of

---

[1] Tzvetan Todorov acknowledges the efficacy of witty reproach as an instrument of reform in *Grammaire du Décaméron*, p. 36.

how man can exert a measure of control over his world (in particular, over its social institutions) through wit. There is a lesson in this for the ten storytelling youths who must return, after their pastoral sojourn to a pestilence-ridden and morally corrupt city prepared to meet its dangers with intelligence and calm. The stories of Day VI continue and refine this theme, while Days VII through IX broaden the lessons of Days I and VI to include situations of all moral shadings.[2] Day X serves as a corrective to the questionable morality of the second half of the *Decameron* with stories of high-minded heroes who vie in magnanimity. Boccaccio ends his *Decameron* on this exalted note of faith in man's power to shape his own destiny and thus releases his *brigata* into the problematic realm of history.

But the *Decameron* contains instances of a world gone awry, in which the protagonists themselves are helpless to act. These occur in Day II as temporal succession, cause and effect, are governed by external forces which exceed human attempts to comprehend or control. Fortune[3] is the umbrella term used in these stories to include all such superior influences, be they historical, economic, or erotic. Protagonists perceive themselves as fortune's thralls, abdicating responsibility for their own lives by positing all causality in superhuman forces.[4] The image of man which emerges from fortune's tale is an inert one, in contrast to the robust, assertive hero who prevails in the bulk of the stories. But Boccaccio cannot long abide such passive examples of humanity, and so throughout Day II he offers glimpses of the active hero who intervenes to shape the outcome of events. Thus, stories of characters who yield to tyrannous fortune, like Madonna Beritola in II, 6, are balanced by ones in which the protagonists triumph over circumstances, as Andreuccio (II, 5) and Alatiel (II, 7) ultimately do.

A study of II, 6 will reveal the human and literary consequences of total surrender to fortune, which in this story stands for the forces of historical change. Political events external to the story-line govern the course of action, setting the plot in motion, precipitating a crisis, and

---

[2] Thomas Greene, in "Forms of Accommodation," sees the "morally ambiguous enterprises" (307) of the second half of the *Decameron* as backhanded affirmations of the social order. See also his pp. 303-304. He reads the stories of Days VII through IX as examples of "hard accommodation" in which traps are sprung and machinations revealed, in contrast to the "soft accommodations" of the rest of the the *Decameron*, where difficult situations are resolved by witty rejoinder, reconciliation, and reunion.

[3] Vincenzo Cioffari, in "The Conception of Fortune in the *Decameron*," *Italica*, 17 (1940), 135, points out the primacy of fortune in the stories of Day II.

[4] Carlo Salinari, instead, sees in Boccaccio's *Fortuna* a humanized force—the personification of a material causality in worldly affairs. See "L'empirismo ideologico del Boccaccio," p. 369.

defining a resolution. It is as if the narrative were a hoop and history the rod used to keep it in motion with timely taps on the rim. Thus, Madonna Beritola's fate is inextricably linked with that of the Ghibelline rule in Sicily. Her husband, Arrighetto Capece, is governor of the island under the reign of the Ghibelline Manfredi, whose claim to the throne is being challenged by the papal favorite, Charles d'Anjou. In the battle of Benevento of 1265, Manfredi is killed, and the Guelfs take over the island of Sicily, putting Ghibelline sympathizers to flight. Arrighetto, however, is among those members of the defeated party who cannot flee the island in time, and so he is imprisoned, while his wife Beritola, their son Guisfredi, and a nurse manage to escape. Beritola gives birth to a second son, Lo Scacciato, on the island of Ponzo, but is abandoned by her entourage when a band of pirates kidnaps everyone but her. The lady is finally rescued by Currado Malaspina and his wife who take her to Lunigiana and keep her in their household disguised as a domestic. Years pass before Guisfredi, under the pseudonym Giannotto, leaves the service of his adoptive lord Guasparrino Doria, joins Currado's household, makes love to Currado's widowed daughter, Spina, and is imprisoned for it. At this juncture, the narrative reaches a deadlock, with Beritola trapped in servitude, Giannotto wasting in jail, Lo Scacciato and his governess relegated to slavery in the household of Guasparrino. The internal momentum of the story has stopped, with no resolution of the tripartite dilemma in sight. Now history intervenes a second time in the form of the Sicilian Vespers of 1282 and reanimates this plot, which has become sluggish to the point of inertia. A political reversal induces the narrative reversal when history and fiction intersect once more to keep the story in motion.

This turn of events precipitates an avalanche of happy endings, as Guisfredi is released from jail, married to la Spina, and reunited with his mother. Lo Scacciato is then freed from his service to Guasparrino, betrothed to his lord's eleven-year-old daughter, and brought to his mother in Lunigiana. Finally, everyone joins Arrighetto in Sicily as the family is restored to its former position of wealth and power. Banquets, swoonings, and rhetorical outbursts mark the various stages of this denouement, with excess reflected in such words as *oltre*, *sopra*, and their compounds. This compulsion to multiply happy endings, to go beyond each phase of the resolution with an even better, more inclusive one, serves to undercut the very idea of resolution, and leaves the reader unconvinced by its finality. The ending seems as arbitrary and as artificially induced as the crisis, which was facilitated by the external agent of history. So it is fitting that the narrator abandon the story to the very forces which generated and motivated its action. "Dove con tanta festa da Arrighetto tutti parimente, e' figliuoli e le donne, furono in Palermo ricevuti, che dir non si potrebbe giammai. Dove poi molto tempo si crede che essi tutti felicemente vivessero" (120).

The reader has no reason to trust the stability of this ending. Why should it be any more conclusive than the previous four, each of which had to be superseded by another, more stupendous one? Also suspicious is the tentative quality of Boccaccio's projections into a future of familial bliss. His insertion of *si crede* and the use of the subjunctive *vivessero* undermine the emphatic assurance of subsequent happiness which such ritual endings customarily imply. We realize, with a measure of disappointment, that the conclusion of this story is as precarious as its beginning, that the protagonists are permanently entrusting themselves to the very forces which destroyed their initial equilibrium and set the narrative in motion: the fickle favor of the Sicilian subjects, and the fluctuations of power among the Guelf and Ghibelline factions. The last line of the tale offers little more hope of stability, placing the fortunes of these protagonists in the hands of a God who resembles more a feudal tyrant than benign providence. Beritola's family pays tribute to this lord "come conoscenti del ricevuto beneficio, amici di messer Domenedio" (120). Earlier, God had been credited with the happy turn of events which restored Arrighetto to power. "Volle Domenedio, abbondantissimo donatore quando comincia, sopragiugnere le liete novelle della vita e del buono stato d'Arrighetto Capece" (119). The qualifier "quando comincia" suggests an uncomfortable analogy between divine providence and a temperamental tyrant who either withholds his favors or squanders them at will. The narrative concludes with an invocation to this capricious lord as we leave the protagonists to the mercy of his erratic good will.

The story ends where it began. History has come full circle, restoring the Ghibellines to power with the Sicilian Vespers in 1282, as it had unseated them at Benevento in 1265. The Sicilian uprising is a revolution in the pure sense of the word, completing the half-turn of the circle that the fall of Manfredi had initiated.[5] The cliché "plus ça change, plus c'est la même chose," could well be the political subtitle of this story. As the narrative reverts to its original position, we realize that the characters have made no linear progress toward greater insight or control, that the experience of seventeen years and eleven pages has landed them right where they began.

[5] In his *Esposizioni sopra la Comedia di Dante*, Boccaccio compares the cyclical movements of fortune to their natural exemplar, the revolutions of the heavenly bodies. See *Tutte le opere di Giovanni Boccaccio*, VI, ed. Giorgio Padoan (Milan, 1965), 399-400.

The story deviates from Boccaccio's standard format in which all the action leads linearly to the climactic moment of wit or illumination and is succeeded by a quick denouement. Instead, we have a denouement which lasts for half the story, creating a symmetrical structure in which the second half of the narrative undoes the action of the first. Each predicament in part one is resolved in the reverse order of its occurrence in part two. Consequently, the initial incident, Arrighetto's imprisonment, is the last to be resolved, while the second, Madonna Beritola's loss of her children, is the penultimate. The enslavement of the sons, the third incident in part one, is the third-to-last to be resolved, and Giannotto's imprisonment, at the center of the story, is the first predicament to be undone after the dramatic reversal.

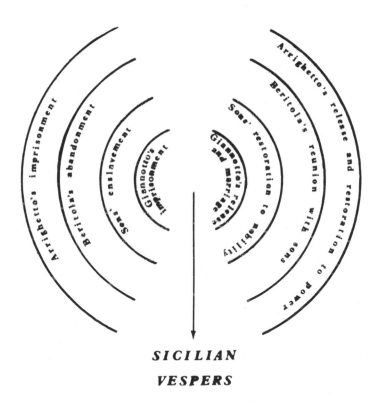

SICILIAN

VESPERS

To enhance the symmetry of this scheme, Boccaccio has made the innermost circle recapitulate the circumference, as the son's year-long imprisonment in Lunigiana is a miniature of his father's seventeen-year captivity in Palermo.

In a similar way, Madonna Beritola's experiences reflect, on a vastly reduced scale, the historical events which circumscribe the story. She has matching fainting spells at the beginning and end of the tale, when she discovers the disappearance of her children and when they are returned to her. In each instance, swooning is described as a kind of death and resurrection, suggesting comparisons with the two political turnabouts of the period: the overthrow of the Ghibellines in 1265 and that of the Guelfs seventeen years later. The characters thus unconsciously reflect the vicissitudes of the events which control them, unable to resist the flux and change of history. As readers, we are also subject to the arbitrary forces which determine the narrative. There is no vantage point beyond the course of events from which we can observe the action with calm and understanding, but instead, we are immersed in the chaos of adventures, deprived of any superior insight which would clarify our reading. In vain we look for a principle of order underlying the fluctuating surface of experience. Finally, when we think we have found a constant in the ideal of nobility, Boccaccio subtly and systematically undermines it, depriving us of any fixed frame of reference.

Although the definition of nobility was a source of lively debate in the Middle Ages, its status as an ontological category was never questioned.[6] Yet Boccaccio does challenge the concept, forcing us to reject nobility as a norm in a narrative world which defies all absolutes. He does this by holding forth the possibility of the noble soul, only to destroy it with a series of logical contradictions. In the case of Giannotto, for example, we are told that beneath a servile façade, his magnanimity remains intact. Indeed, there seems to be a constant tension between his great spirit and the mean trappings which fortune compels him to wear. He chafes at the servant's life, "avendo più animo che a servo non s'apparteneva, sdegnando la viltà della servil condizione" (113). Later, the luminosity of his soul shines through his wasted flesh in jail ("aveva la prigione macerate le carni di Giannotto, ma il generoso animo dalla sua origine tratto non aveva ella in cosa alcuna diminuito") (116), making imprisonment a metaphor for the confinement of a noble soul in a paltry container. Currado, too, is finally impressed with Giannotto's greatness of spirit, "avendo costui udito, si maravigliò e di grande animo il tenne" (116). Boccaccio is

---

[6] Andreas Capellanus, whose treatise on courtly love is patterned on the medieval hierarchy of social classes, is thoroughly obsessed with the idea of nobility. The interlocutors of his eight model dialogues are exclusively identified by their positions in the social structure, and the issue of nobility weaves in and out of their conversations. See Andreas Capellanus, *The Art of Courtly Love*, trans. John Jay Parry (New York, 1969), p. 35, in particular.

apparently setting forth the proposition that inner virtue is an absolute which the vicissitudes of accident and chance cannot hide. But the facts of the story soon destroy his conviction, for Currado does not recognize Giannotto's nobility until after he has been informed of his prisoner's identity. The protagonist's great soul thus makes its appearance only when Currado knows to look for it. His nobility has no absolute existence; it is contingent on the consensus of a fickle world.

Boccaccio also suggests that Giannotto lacks the inner virtue which would render him noble despite society's ignorance. We are not told why his excursion to Alexandria ends in failure, but are left entertaining unflattering ideas about the young man's competence to deal with the world. The conduct of Giannotto's love affair with La Spina also leaves much to be desired. Not only is he careless and stupid, oblivious to her good name, but he also violates one of the cardinal rules of courtly conduct, for Andreas Capellanus makes secrecy the cornerstone of his code, and assigns the harshest punishments to its transgressors.[7] In his indiscreet management of the affair with La Spina, Giannotto is not only exposed as a fornicator, but as a violator of the Chaplain's golden rule.

It is not surprising, then, that nobody recognizes Giannotto's inner nobility, for he is lacking in the virtues which would make that attribute shine through his ignoble disguise. Not even his mother identifies him despite occasional contact in the Malaspina household, for it is only after Currado formally introduces one to the other that they sense their kinship, she by "occulta vertu" (117), and he by "l'odor materno" (117). Until now, each has judged the other by appearance alone, never motivated to probe beyond the mean surface of servile disguise. Only when their true identities are revealed do the "occulta vertu" and the "odor materno" become evident, thus negating the very notion of hidden powers and the privileged knowledge which such powers confer. Giannotto and Beritola see each other strictly through the eyes of the world, and their perspective can only change when the world itself begins to see differently.

The notion of inner nobility is most effectively refuted by Beritola herself. Her sojourn in the state of nature, as she awaits rescue on the island of Ponzo, becomes a biting satire on a society which predicates itself on the finest gradations of rank and birth. It is the day after the kidnapping of her children by pirates, and as Beritola wanders about her new island home, she happens upon a cave inhabited by a family of roe-deer. Though Boccaccio never makes it explicit, this mother deer and her two newborn fawns must remind the lady of her own

---

[7] The Chaplain's imperatives to secrecy are emphatic. See his pp. 34 and 185.

family, now dispersed throughout the Mediterranean. The sight of the two tiny animals brings out Beritola's tenderest maternal instincts—"le parevano la più dolce cosa del mondo e la più vezzosa" (111)—and since her breasts are still heavy with milk from the recent birth of her own baby, she suckles the newborn fawns. So satisfactory is this arrangement that Beritola becomes one of the family, grazing, watering, and lodging with her new "compagnia" (111).

Not only does the peacefulness and attractiveness of this idyllic interlude put a warlike world to shame, but so too does the fact that the hierarchical structure of human society is totally negated by the egalitarianism of nature, which subjects man and beast to the same laws of survival. Thus the baby roe-deer make no distinction between their natural mother and their surrogate one: "dalla madre a lei niuna distinzion fecero" (111), while Beritola herself feels as comfortable with her animal step-children as with her own offspring. Boccaccio delivers the greatest blow to civilized society in Beritola's absolute reluctance to leave the company of roe-deer and the island retreat when Currado and his wife beg her to join them in returning to Lunigiana. Their difficulty in convincing the lady to leave bespeaks as much the attractiveness of this natural state as Beritola's resolve to mourn her family's loss by living and dying on the island.

It takes very little to bring out the animal in Madonna Beritola, and with the slightest change of spelling, the name Beritola Caracciola becomes Beritola Cavriuola. The lady's first meal on the island is described by the verb *pascere*, not *mangiare* ("a pascer l'erbe si diede" 111), implying the animal turn her life is about to take. Boccaccio uses this easy transition from gentlewoman to beast to further degrade the notion of social caste. It is significant that Beritola undergoes her metamorphosis on an island, for in the absence of a community to define her elitist position, the lady easily slips into animal ways. She is entirely determined by her setting, and now that the context is natural, her identity modifies accordingly. Nobility thus becomes an external attribute, as superficial and precarious as all the other elements in the story. Beritola cannot express her true status until the political situation itself changes, and without external manifestation of her identity, it ceases to exist and is easily replaced by others: first bestial, and then servile. Like power and wealth, nobility is thus reduced to the accidental and the contingent.

Paradoxically, the only absolute in the story is fortune herself. Once we have identified this as the operant force of the narrative, a vast body of medieval lore can be invoked to explain the dynamics of the story. Its cyclical plot has an exact iconographic equivalent in the wheel of fortune which governs the shifting movements of material goods, as H.R. Patch describes them: "The wheel, then, in the Middle Ages means relative exaltation or humiliation in worldly dignity. It is turned by Fortuna and man is often actually attached to the rim, where he suffers the consequent changes of position."[8] Of great relevance to our story is a refinement of this motif which graphs fortune's transfers of power, using the emblem of the wheel surrounded by four figures to illustrate the captions *regno, regnavi, sum sine regno*, and *regnabo*.[9] Boccaccio's readers must surely have visualized this motif as they read of the waxing and waning fortunes of the Ghibelline cause, incarnated in the figure of Arrighetto Capece.[10]

Structurally, many of the tales in Day II are patterned on the wheel of fortune. The count of Antwerp rises, falls, and rises again as the wheel goes through one complete revolution in II, 8. Susan Clark and Julian Wasserman have shown how the wheel makes two complete turns in the water-logged adventures of Landolfo Rufolo (II, 4).[11] But in several other tales, the relationship between the protagonists and the wheel changes dramatically. In these cases the protagonists begin as victims, but end by seizing control of the wheel and stopping its fatal turning. Andreuccio of Perugia (II, 5), initially the dupe of both man and circumstance, becomes an accomplished opportunist, while Alatiel (II, 7) learns cunning and stops the wheel at its apex. Thus, though Day II promises to give as passive and submissive an image of man as any in the *Decameron*, Boccaccio already offers us an alternative in the Andreuccios and Alatiels who come to play an active role in the shaping of their narrations.

If the tale of Madonna Beritola is a historical romance, where fortune assumes the guise of history as the motivating force of the story line, a similar analysis will reveal in the tale of Andreuccio a mercantile romance, where a business transaction subtends the plot. In the adventures of Andreuccio, Boccaccio is poking fun at the retail system which prolongs the interval between the beginning and the end of a commercial exchange, and populates that distance with middlemen who profit from superior access to consumer products. Andreuccio is

[8] H.R. Patch, *The Goddess Fortuna in Mediaeval Literature* (Cambridge, Mass., 1927), p. 159.
[9] Ibid., p. 164.
[10] Boccaccio discusses the wheel-like quality of fortune's operations in his *Esposizioni sopra la Comedia di Dante*, p. 398. Elsewhere, he makes use of the wheel of fortune, for example, in *De casibus virorum illustrium* we read that the Angevin King Charles, who figures importantly in the background history of *Decameron* II, 6, has a cyclical rise and fall from power. See Giovanni Boccaccio, *Opere in versi, Corbaccio, Trattatello in laude di Dante, Prose latine, Epistole*, ed. Pier Giorgio Ricci (Milan, 1965), p. 842.
[11] Susan Clark and Julian Wasserman, "*Decameron* II, 4: The Journey of the Hero," *Mediaevalia*, 3 (Fall 1977), 1-16.

such a middleman, a horse dealer who comes to Naples to buy
wholesale what he will then sell at a profit in Perugia. But this potential retailer falls victim to the very commercial practices which he
uncritically accepts, when buyer, seller, and merchandise all become
confused in one murky Neapolitan night.[12]

Even at the beginning of the story, Andreuccio seems to be having
trouble transacting business. In the hustle and bustle of the marketplace, he finds no lack of eligible horses, but is unable to conclude
any deals. It is obvious that the Neapolitan salesmen spot him as an
easy dupe and refuse to budge on their asking prices. To make matters worse, Andreuccio feels he must show off his 500 florins and
convince the Neapolitans that he means business. By flaunting his
capital, the Perugian not only reveals his limitless naiveté, but also
forfeits his bargaining power. For the salesmen know exactly what
Andreuccio can afford and will set their prices accordingly. Now it is
no longer the horses which are on the market, but Andreuccio's
purse, and the Neapolitans can decide how cheaply it may be won.
The buyer's and seller's roles have thus been reversed—a reversal
which will be even more evident in the encounter with the Sicilian
prostitute, Madama Fiordaliso.[13] Herself a marketable item, this lady is
"disposta per piccol pregio a compiacere a qualunque uomo" (98). But
now it is Andreuccio who is for sale, and she the buyer of his un-
guarded assets; her capital: a winning smile and a good story whose
counterfeit nature the protagonist never suspects. Ignorant of what
he must pay for this transaction, Andreuccio is happy with his share in
it. Not only is this "long lost sister" a sentimental gain, but her supposed wealth adds to his own sense of prestige. "E nel vero, io non
conosco uomo di sì alto affare, al quale voi non doveste esser cara, non
che a me che un picciolo mercatante sono" (101).[14] In his own estima-
tion, Andreuccio is elevated from the level of a petty broker to the
imagined status of a great merchant by the acquisition of a sister who
is both rich and nobly married. Little suspecting the depths to which
he will soon plunge, Andreuccio is about to lose not only this im-

[12] For the classic study of the importance of the Neapolitan setting of this tale, see
Benedetto Croce, "La novella di Andreuccio da Perugia," in *Storie e leggende napoletane*
(Bari, 1959), pp. 45-84.
[13] For a syntactic analysis of the two long periods within which these events are told, see
Fredi Chiappelli, "Sul linguaggio del Sannazzaro," *Vox romanica*, 13 (1953), 46-47. The
interpenetration of amorous and economic motifs in this opening sequence is subtly
and thoroughly analyzed by Getto, *Vita di forme*, pp. 84-85.
[14] Greg Lucente sees in this comment proof that Andreuccio has fallen for la Siciliana's
double bait: her appeal to his lust and to his cupidity. See "The Fortunate Fall of
Andreuccio da Perugia," *Forum italicum*, 10, n. 4 (1976), 327.

agined prestige, but his actual capital of 500 florins.[15] This, however, does not stop him from having real value in the eyes of two grave robbers who make Andreuccio an accessory in their scheme to rob the tomb of the archbishop, Filippo Minutolo. Whether out of a certain respect for the dead, or out of their own aesthetic sense, the grave robbers decide first to cleanse Andreuccio of the traces of his recent fall. No sooner is he lowered into a well than two night watchmen approach for water and frighten the thieves away. Andreuccio is hoisted up out of the well by the unwitting guards whose thirst gives way to fear at the sight of a man at the end of the rope in place of a bucket. Abandoned by the fleeing guards, Andreuccio is soon rejoined by the two thieves who proceed with him to the site of the archbishop's tomb.

During the grave robbery, Andreuccio plays the middleman in a very literal sense, transferring the riches from the tomb to the pockets of his colleagues outside. As recompense for his pains, the protagonist makes a handsome profit by withholding the archbishop's ruby ring from his two accomplices. Now the business deal is complete and Andreuccio returns to Perugia the next day with a precious jewel worth somewhat more than his original 500 florins. In the final line of the tale, Boccaccio transcribes the bizarre events of this Neapolitan night into a kind of commercial shorthand, identifying only the terminal points of the transaction, "a Perugia tornossi, avendo il suo investito in uno anello, dove per comperare cavalli era andato" (108). The story thus resides in the multiplication of steps which intervene between the beginning and the end of a business exchange, making the narration analogous to the commercial process itself, wherein middlemen occupy the interval between production and consumption.[16] Perugia, the geographical butt of the tale, is itself a middleman among cities. Strategically located in Umbria, Perugia was and is an ideal trade center whose economy derives from the bringing together of buyers and sellers.

In Andreuccio's three falls, Greg Lucente finds a systematic and coherent religious parody.[17] But there is another iconographic system at work here as well. The wheel of fortune, whose ceaseless turning

[15] Aldo Rossi notes the irony in the fact that Andreuccio "pays" 500 florins yet never enjoys the embraces of a woman who is disposed to sell herself for much less. See "La combinatoria decameroniana: Andreuccio," *Strumenti critici*, 7 (February 1973), 30.

[16] Though Getto considers "la realtà economica" the framing motif of the story, providing a beginning and an end to the plot (*Vita di forme*, p. 94), he denies its central importance to the meaning of the tale. I believe, however, that the commercial element is crucial to the overall satiric effect of the story and that a systematic spoof of the mercantile process can be traced throughout.

[17] Greg Lucente, "The Fortunate Fall," pp. 337-338.

serves to reallocate material wealth, has a special place in the mercantile romance. For Dante, the unstable and fluctuating distribution of worldly goods is the quintessential example of fortune's dominion over human affairs. It is the spectacle of the misers and spendthrifts in *Inferno* VII, moving in their half circles, crashing against each other with huge weights, which prompts Dante to ask Virgil a leading question about the theological status of fortune. Virgil echoes Boethius in asserting that fortune is an agent of divine providence, continually shifting the distribution of material wealth according to the dictates of God's master plan:

> a li splendor mondani
> ordinò general ministra e duce
> che permutasse a tempo li ben vani
> di gente in gente e d'uno in altro sangue
> oltre la difension di senni umani.
> (*Inf.* VII, 77-81)

Unlike the characters in II,6 who passively submit to fortune's blows, Andreuccio helps her administer them. The tale may be seen as a *Bildungsroman* wherein the hero falls once, twice, even three times, but rises to never fall again. By now Andreuccio is so well versed in the strategies of fortune that he can use them to his own advantage. Therefore, when the robbers lower him into the archbishop's tomb, he is able to second-guess their duplicity. "Costoro mi ci fanno entrare per ingannarmi, per ciò che, come io avrò loro ogni cosa dato, mentre che io penerò a uscir dall'arca, essi se ne andranno pe' fatti loro e io rimarrò senza cosa alcuna" (107). Having discerned the robbers' real motives, Andreuccio decides to fight fraud with fraud: "e per ciò s'avisò di farsi innanzi tratto la parte sua; e ricordatosi del caro anello che aveva loro udito dire, come fu giù disceso, così di dito il trasse all'arcivescovo e miselo a sé; e poi dato il pasturale e la mitra e' guanti e spogliatolo infino alla camiscia, ogni cosa diè loro dicendo che più niente v'avea" (107). But this trick is not enough to right Andreuccio's position on the wheel of fortune. It will take another contrivance to free him from danger as the robbers seal him in the tomb and a new band of thieves, this time led by a priest, comes in to despoil the corpse of the archbishop. This second group, however, is plagued by a fear of the rapacious dead, and Andreuccio takes his cue from their credulity. No sooner does the leader assure his colleagues that the dead don't attack, than Andreuccio does exactly that—grabbing the priest's leg and pretending to pull him into the tomb. This gesture is a measure of just how far the protagonist has traveled on his journey into the wisdom of the world. Originally the dupe of false appearances, Andreuccio now knows how to manipulate them for his own ends. As he leaps up out of the tomb, polishing his ruby ring, the protagonist is literally a man reborn—in league with Lady Fortune where he had once been her choicest victim.[18]

Another of Boccaccio's protagonists who remains "fortune's plaything" until the very end of her saga is Alatiel, the winsome heroine of II, 7.[19] Like Andreuccio, she learns cunning and is able to control the operations of fortune which had once kept her so helplessly captive. As Andreuccio's tale was a long parenthesis in the commerical process, so hers is a long detour in a nuptial journey. The narrative begins as Alatiel sets off for the realm of Algarve, whose king she is to wed. Prosperous winds lead the ship to within sight of its destination, "parendo loro [ai marinari] alla fine del loro cammino esser vicini" (122), but the end is to be indefinitely postponed as a violent storm sends the boat, and the narrative, on a many years' digression which will constitute the bulk of the story. Alatiel is rendered helpless, first by the turbulent sea, and then by the turbulent passions she arouses in her male admirers.[20] During this four-year vacation from virtue, Alatiel makes a tour of the Mediterranean world, leaving in her wake a trail of dead lovers, broken families, internecine wars, and betrayed trust. Herself too ineffectual to do evil, Alatiel seems to bring out the evil in her suitors, causing them to engage in any and all antisocial behaviors to win her.

Alatiel's odyssey has not only sexual and political, but also economic implications, for her itinerary approximates the medieval trade routes of the Mediterranean world.[21] Victor Šklovsky's argument that Boccaccio's novelty inheres in new attitudes towards old material[22] could be well substantiated by the saga of Alatiel. The plot harks back to the archetypal Greek romance of the beautiful young

---

[18] Carlo Muscetta, in *Giovanni Boccaccio* (Bari, 1972), sees the ruby ring as the emblem of Fortune's new partnership with Andreuccio. "La chiusa è d'una poeticità e di una semplicità magistrale, e salda la struttura anulare del racconto sulla gemma in cui sembra fiammeggiare l'amuleto della fortuna amica" (198).

[19] Mario Baratto sees in Alatiel not only a "trastullo della fortuna" but also a plaything of the storyteller in Boccaccio's desire to place her in countless situations which produce the same mechanical chain of results. See *Realtà e stile*, pp. 96-100.

[20] Hauvette interprets this tale as "une sorte d'hymne à la puissance tragique de l'amour" though he himself is quick to point out the irony of the fact that Alatiel makes little resistance to seduction and seems to enjoy her subjugation to the God of Love—an irony which would militate against any tragic reading of her tale. See *Boccace*, pp. 264-265.

[21] For this observation, I am indebted to my student Don Kothman whose research on Boccaccio's attitude toward the medieval East revealed the commercial ramifications of Alatiel's travels. Branca, however, gives another logic to the itinerary of her journey: "le vicende dei principi angioini in Morea," and "l'avventuroso viaggio di Niccolò Acciaiuoli fra il '38 e il '41." See *Boccaccio medievale*, p. 147.

[22] This is a recurrent theme in Šklovsky's *Lettura del 'Decameron.'*

woman who is passed about from hand to hand but never sullied. What occurred under the aegis of the gods in Greek romance now occurs under the impulse of commercial gain in Boccaccio.[23] This change in governing forces may well explain why Boccaccio's protagonist is anything but the monotonously chaste heroine of Greek romance. She is a mercantile commodity, transferred from port to port and literally consumed by her various possessors. If her travels are to be emblematic of the flow of goods in a commercial system, then of course Alatiel must be used and enjoyed by the many consumers into whose hands and beds she will fall.[24]

Not surprisingly, each of her ports of arrival is a prominent trade center and she herself is handed about as the most valuable of commodities: a beautiful woman with a pedigree. Indeed, this second quality contributes as much as the first to her market value, making Alatiel an asset to her lovers' social as well as sexual vanity. Thus Pericone, Alatiel's host on the island of Majorca, and her initiator into the joys of the flesh, notices first the signs of her noble origin, and only then her beauty. "Comprese, per gli arnesi ricchi la donna che trovata avea dovere essere gran gentil donna, e lei prestamente conobbe all'onore che vedeva dall'altre fare a lei sola" (124). The prince of Morea's ardor doubles in intensity when he discovers that his beloved is obviously an aristocrat. "Il prenze vedendola oltre alla bellezza ornata di costumi reali, non potendo altramenti saper chi ella si fosse, nobile donna dovere essere la stimò e pertanto il suo amore in lei si raddoppiò" (127). The possession of so comely and well-born a mistress enhances her lovers in the eyes of the world, and their desire to enjoy this prestige leads the men to their fatal mistake: showing her off before an admiring, but lethal public. Thus, when the duke of Athens challenges the prince of Morea to prove that Alatiel's beauty lives up to its reputation, the prince is only too happy to oblige. Yet by flaunting Alatiel's beauty before his friend, the prince is signing his own death warrant. The duke of Athens accordingly murders his rival, abducts the lady, but only to commit his predecessor's fatal mistake in showing off his prize to Alatiel's next abductor. Consequently, when Constanzio begs the duke to let him behold the lady's charms, the latter gladly consents, "mal ricordandosi di ciò che al prenze avvenuto era per averla mostrata a lui" (131). History repeats itself as Constanzio takes from the duke what he in turn had taken

---

[23] Ibid., p. 222.
[24] In this commercial analogy, Giancarlo Mazzacurati sees Branca's notion of the "epopea mercantile" reflected not only on the level of narrative content, but on a deeper, structural level—that is the "principio di relazione tra i suoi oggetti." See *Forma e ideologia*, p. 54.

from the prince. So great a social asset is Alatiel that her possessors cannot resist publicly exhibiting the lady's charms, despite the dangers of such inflammatory beauty.

Two things conspire to rob Alatiel of her humanity and reduce her to the level of mere ornament: first, her suitors do not know who she is, and second, they share no medium of communication with her. Without language, Alatiel's admirers can only respond to her in a physical way. She ceases to be a human being, as complicated and as multifaceted as themselves, and serves instead as a screen onto which their own sexual desires may be projected. Alatiel becomes the nameless and selfless partner of pornographic fantasy who makes no emotional demands on her mates and frees them of all moral responsibility for their desires.

Although Panfilo, in his didactic introduction to the tale, blames Alatiel's misadventures on her excessive beauty, it is her speechlessness which makes her the quintessential "trastullo della fortuna" (135).[25] Wordlessly she gives in to Pericone's desires and wordlessly she is consoled by successive lovers for the loss of each preceding one. Without language Alatiel loses the faculty of memory: unable to preserve past experience in her mind with words, she forgets vows of chastity, past lovers, her own identity, and the very purpose of her journey. And since wordlessness condemns her to the tyrannous rule of fortune, it is only through language that she can once more gain control of her destiny. This she does with the help of Antigono, a member of her father's court whom she meets on the island of Cyprus. The courtier, who ultimately recognizes Alatiel as the daughter of the sultan, does not add his name to the list of lovers, but instead helps her devise a clever story to cleanse her sin-stained past. Alatiel is brought home to Alexandria where she recites this alibi to her father and persuades him that the four "lost" years were spent in the safety of a convent. Convinced, the sultan sends his daughter off to the king of Algarve who accepts this oft-enjoyed lady as his virgin bride.

Through the resumption of language, Alatiel has not only regained her identity, but erased a disreputable past. Now the nuptial voyage, so long delayed by storms, passions, and intrigues, is finally brought to completion. The concluding proverb recapitulates the cyclical structure of this tale, whose ending matches its beginning and whose middle is effectively annulled. "Bocca basciata non perde ventura, anzi rinnuova come fa la luna" (140). In the moon, Boccaccio has chosen not only the astronomical symbol of the female reproductive cycle,

---

[25] For a more intensive treatment of this theme, the reader is referred to my study, "Seduction by Silence: A Gloss on the Tales of Masetto (III, 1) and Alatiel (II, 7)," to appear in *Philological Quarterly*.

but the perfect analogue for the temporality of this tale—as the moon is renewed monthly, so Alatiel "revirginates"[26] at the end of the story, thus annihilating the experience of long wanderings and countless coitions. In the lunar waxing and waning of this lady's adventures, we may also discern the movements of the wheel of fortune—the structural motif common to so many of the tales in the second day. Yet it is Alatiel herself who brings the wheel full circle at the conclusion of her story. Through the help of Antigone she "rewrites" her adventures and casts them in a variant form acceptable to father and bridegroom. Thus she is able to hoist herself back up to the top of the wheel of fortune and maintain herself there through the exercise of cunning self-assertion. No longer the passive object of male sexual desire, nor the victim of the unpredictable sea in which Boccaccio has literalized the metaphoric *fluctus concupiscentiae*, Alatiel is now in charge of her destiny. Like Andreuccio, she has progressed from the status of fortune's plaything to fortune's accomplice as the wheel's fatal turning is finally stilled.

Structurally, all three of the tales discussed above share several common elements besides the imagery of the wheel. In each of these stories the sequence of events is arbitrarily determined by factors external to the story-line. The action does not unfold according to any internal laws of necessity or probability, but demonstrates instead the strictly non-Aristotelian poetic of medieval romance as Eugene Vinaver describes it.[27] Accordingly, these plots consist of an infinitely expandable series of events and bear none of the formal properties which modern readers associate with narrative unity: a beginning, middle, and end organically related to form a coherent whole. Madonna Beritola's family could undergo another installment of mishaps—for example, Lo Scacciato's adventures could be developed—without influencing the outcome of the narration. Similarly, Andreuccio's saga could be lengthened or shortened without altering the resolution. In fact, Pasolini inexplicably deletes the episode at the well from his filmed version of this tale with no loss of dramatic effect. Whether Alatiel's list of lovers is expanded or contracted is a matter of indifference to the resolution of II, 7. Her story may be seen as a series of variations on the theme: abduction, seduction, abduction. An endless number of such episodes could be envisioned, though fortunately for us, Boccaccio limits himself to nine.

---

[26] I am indebted to Stavros Deligiorgis for this neologism. See *Narrative Intellection in the 'Decameron'* (Iowa City, 1975), p. 38.

[27] Eugene Vinaver, *The Rise of Romance* (New York and Oxford, 1971). For a masterful analysis of the medieval romance aesthetic, see his chapter "The Poetry of Interlace," pp. 68-98.

The arbitrariness of all these plots reflects on a structural level the caprice of fortune's rule, making the tales formal examples of the very world view they espouse.

Yet there are some structural differences among the tales worth noting. The happy ending of Madonna Beritola's ordeal is far less stable than those of the other two tales. Historical circumstance, which presides over Beritola's final good fortune, gives no assurance of permanence. But since Alatiel and Andreuccio have taken matters into their own hands, the resolutions of their stories offer greater promise of stability. These protagonists have managed to escape the arbitrariness of the romantic mode by finally intervening to determine the outcome of their plots. Andreuccio does so by anticipating subsequent events and co-opting them. Alatiel does so in a much more momentous way: by literally rewriting her story. This revision constitutes an internal criticism of her tale, exposing the inadequacy of a plot which consists of a possibly endless series of variations on a theme. Alatiel's revised narration does away with such serial repetitions and introduces a linear story line with coherent beginning, middle, and end. By rewriting her past, as did Ser Ciappelletto and Andreuccio's Sicilian prostitute, Alatiel literally becomes the author of her destiny, bringing about the happy ending so unwarranted by her "real" adventures on the stormy Mediterranean Sea.

Thus, within Day II, where fortune should reign supreme, Boccaccio subverts that dictatorship by introducing characters who ultimately refuse to submit to the forces of accident and chance.[28] In their belated efforts to influence events, these characters rescue their plots from the circumstantial and confer a measure of stability on their resolutions. Despite the equivocal morality of the Andreuccios and the Alatiels of Day II, it is they who will prevail in the world of the *Decameron*, and not the Beritolas and the Arrighettos who passively await fortune's next blow and invite their own extinction.

---

[28] As R. Hastings points out in *Nature and Reason*, p. 95, Boccaccio's endorsement of human initiative in the wake of misfortune is proved by the themes of Days III and VI which celebrate industry and wit. On the same subject, see his pp. 101-102.

III

TRAGEDY AS TRESPASS

THE TALE OF TANCREDI AND GHISMONDA (IV, 1)

It is not by accident that one of the protagonists of Boccaccio's first tragic tale is a tyrant. Not only is the theory of love which wreaks havoc on the lives of Tancredi, Ghismonda, and Guiscardo a despotic one, but so is the tale itself which exerts over its readers a relentless and inexorable power. In the opening passage, Boccaccio reveals to us the harsh end of his tale, making his narration tyrannous in its inevitability. "Tancredi, prencipe di Salerno, fu signore assai umano e di benigno ingegno, se egli nell'amoroso sangue nella sua vecchiezza non s'avesse le mani bruttate" (267). The reader knows from the start that Tancredi will murder for love. In the very next period, Boccaccio discloses who one of his victims will be.[1] "Il quale in tutto lo spazio della sua vita non ebbe che una figliuola, e più felice sarebbe stato se quella avuta non avesse" (267). This striking insertion of an authorial judgment ("più felice sarebbe stato se quella avuta non avesse") connects the description of Tancredi's daughter with the previous prophecy of murder. It is not long before the reader learns the motivation for so cruel a crime when Boccaccio describes the possessive love borne by this father toward his only child. "Costei fu dal padre tanto teneramente amata quanto alcuna altra figliuola da padre fosse giammai, e per questo tenero amore, avendo ella di molti anni avanzata l'età del dovere avere avuto marito, non sappiendola da sé partire, non la maritava" (267). We may wonder if Boccaccio is not hinting at a more-than-paternal affection when he repeats the descriptive "tenero" in its variant "teneramente" twice in the very passage which

---

[1] Although Tancredi is not directly responsible for Ghismonda's death, his actions necessitate her suicide. The tragic consequences of his repressive love will be discussed further on.

44

asserts Tancredi's reluctance to give his daughter in marriage.[2] This oft repeated descriptive will meet its counterpart in forms of the verb *incrudelire* throughout the second part of the tale. Indeed, the initial excess of paternal love is a measure of the anger and hate which will propel Tancredi to his murderous act of revenge.

When the prince finally does arrange for Ghismonda to marry, her bliss is short-lived, for the son of the duke of Capua, her husband, dies soon after the nuptial event: "Poi alla fine a un figliuolo del duca di Capova datala, poco tempo dimorata con lui, rimase vedova e al padre tornossi" (267). Boccaccio matches the brevity of Ghismonda's marriage with the economy of his syntax, compressing Tancredi's betrothal of his daughter into the participial composite "datala" and limiting her marital sojourn to the confines of the five-word phrase "poco tempo dimorata con lui." To a medieval reader, however, the implications of Ghismonda's short acquaintance with conjugal life would not be lost. Widows were notorious in the Middle Ages for their desire to resume the carnal delights of their previous marital state.[3] Hence, the Wife of Bath's serial partners in the institution she could never quite bring herself to abandon. Later, Ghismonda will invoke the medieval lore about widows to justify her adultery, characterizing herself as "piena di concupiscibile disidero, al quale maravigliosissime forze hanno date l'aver già, per essere stato maritata, conosciuto qual piacer sia a così fatto disidero dar compimento" (271).

Indeed Ghismonda is made for love. She is "bellissima del corpo e del viso quanto alcuna altra femina fosse mai" (267). A similar hyperbolic construction describes Tancredi's affection for his daughter, "tanto teneramente amata, quanto alcuna altra figliuola da padre fosse giammai." These two hyperbolic statements reveal the dilemma of Ghismonda, caught as she is between the excess of paternal love on the one hand, and her own predisposition to adult passion on the other. For a while, she acquiesces to her father's will, playing the role of wife-surrogate perhaps too well: "dimorando col tenero padre, sì come gran donna, in molte dilicatezze" (267). But Ghismonda decides to take matters into her own hands when she despairs of Tancredi's consent to arrange a second marriage. After a systematic investigation

---

[2] After having written this essay, I read Mario Baratto's careful analysis of the tale of Tancredi and Ghismonda in *Realtà e stile nel 'Decameron'* and found that his interpretation coincides with mine on several points. He, too, notes the insistence on the "tenderness" of this father-daughter love and suggests its morbid quality (p. 185). Other points of agreement between Baratto's interpretation and mine will be noted in the following pages.

[3] For Boccaccio's explicit statement on the sexual needs of widows, see Osgood, *Boccaccio on Poetry*, p. 68.

*ghis' reversal of sex roles
" self. awareness/consuientious choice

of all likely young men at court, Ghismonda finally chooses Guiscardo, a man of low birth but exceptional virtue, to be her lover.

In this opening passage, then, Boccaccio has given us all the prerequisites for tragedy. We know the murderous conclusion from the
very start, and we know the *who* and the *why* of this tragic necessity. It
remains for us only to see how events unfold to produce the preor-
dained end. And lest we be distracted by the young lovers' dalliance
and forget that this is a tragedy, Boccaccio intercedes with a dire
warning midway into the story: "Ma la fortuna, invidiosa di così lungo
e di così gran diletto, con doloroso avvenimento la letizia de' due
amanti rivolse in tristo pianto" (269). As readers, we are caught in this
tragic circle, unable to escape the conclusion which we have anticipated from the very start. In its urgency and inevitability, the tale of
Tancredi and Ghismonda exhibits the very tryanny which characterizes their death-dealing loves.

Though all three of the protagonists are driven by amorous passion, Tancredi's is of an utterly unconscious sort, while the young
couple's is deliberate and well considered. The high degree of self-
awareness which typifies all of Ghismonda's acts governs the conduct
of her love as well. Though we may be astonished at the extremely
calculating and intellectual way in which she chooses a lover, Ghismonda is following the dictates of Andreas Capellanus to perfection.
Her choice of Guiscardo, based on ethical considerations, illustrates
the very logic of Andreas's arguments for the superiority of adultery
over matrimony. Since marriage partners are bound by contract to
gratify each other's desires, they are not free to reward probity with
love as adulterers can.[4] This Ghismonda does, and she proceeds according to the four steps prescribed by Andreas in his *De arte honeste
amandi*. For reasons which will be considered later, Ghismonda only
deviates from this code in her reversal of the sex roles assigned to the
knight and the lady. Thus, Ghismonda takes the first step in courtly
love when she singles out Guiscardo for his excellence, and "spesso
vedendolo, fieramente s'accese, ognora più lodando i modi suoi"
(268). With the roles reversed, this corresponds to the onset of love in
Andreas's courtly code. "For when a man sees some woman fit for love
and shaped according to his taste, he begins at once to lust after her in
his heart."[5] Andreas's model lover now internalizes the idea of his
lady, imagines her naked body and "desires to put each part of it to
the fullest use." Likewise, Ghismonda wishes above all else the fulfill-

[4] See Andreas Capellanus, *The Art of Courtly Love*, pp. 106-107.
[5] Ibid., p. 29. The following steps in Andreas' inception of love are all to be found on
this same page of his treatise.

ment of imagined embraces, "niuna altra cosa tanto disiderando la giovane quanto di ritrovarsi con lui" (268). Now Andreas's exemplary lover seeks an intercessor ("straightway he strives to get a helper and to find an intermediary"), but Ghismonda dare not take such a risk, "né vogliendosi di questo amore in alcuna persona fidare" (268); however, like Andreas's model, who plots a meeting ("he begins to seek a place and a time opportune for talking"), Ghismonda similarly contrives "una nuova malizia. Essa scrisse una lettera, e in quella ciò che a fare il dì seguente per esser con lei gli mostrò" (268). Of course, Ghismonda and Guiscardo are most obedient to Andreas's code in their stealth, following with painstaking care his thirteenth law of love ("when made public love rarely endures").[6] Every event of this first half of the tale is cloaked in secrecy,[7] from Ghismonda's decision to take a lover "occultamente" (267) to the lovers' hidden glances, "amando l'un l'altro segretamente" (268) to the tunnel which Ghismonda finds hidden in a nearby hillside that connects to her bedchamber by "una segreta scala" (268), allowing for the fulfillment of their amorous desires through "discreto ordine . . . acciò che segreti fossero" (269).

The lovers have long been enjoying the fruits of their hidden arrangement when Tancredi surprises them *in flagrante*. But the manner of Tancredi's discovery reveals his own complicity in passion, for he has stolen into his daughter's bedroom, as secretly as any lover, "quasi come se studiosamente si fosse nascoso" (269). Boccaccio's locution "quasi come se" suggests Tancredi's unconscious enactment of Andreas's imperative to secrecy. As Guido Almansi comments on the erotic implications of Tancredi's bedside manner, "this seems in absolute terms a superb model of an unconfessed love sentiment. The old man who falls asleep with his head leant against the empty bed of his daughter suggests a whole area of unconscious personal feelings."[8] We also learn that such secret entrances into Ghismonda's bedchamber are not unusual with Tancredi, who thinks nothing of violating his daughter's privacy at whim: "Era usato Tancredi di venirsene alcuna volta tutto solo nella camera della figliuola" (269). The same idiom is used to describe the lovers' amorous routine, "e andatisene in su il letto, sì come usati erano" (269). Both Tancredi and Guiscardo are accustomed to the same degree of intimacy with Ghismonda—a

[6] Ibid., p. 185.
[7] Getto aptly points out the subterranean quality of the entire amorous intrigue. See "La novella di Ghismonda e la struttura della quarta giornata," in *Vita di forme e forme di vita nel 'Decameron,'* pp. 105, 106.
[8] See Almansi, *The Writer as Liar*, p. 143. For Baratto's interpretation of this incestuous moment, see *Realtà e stile*, p. 187.

coincidence which cannot help but someday lead to exposure. Thus, we would be wrong to attribute Tancredi's discovery of the liaison to pure chance,[9] for the very liberties which the prince takes with his daughter are so much like a lover's that the rivalry is bound to surface.

Tancredi's identity as a competitor in love is sealed by a comparison with another, remarkably similar, story of jealousy and revenge. This is the tale of Guiglielmo Rossiglione and Guiglielmo Guardastagno (IV, 9) in which a wronged husband tears out the heart of his murdered rival and serves it to his wife for dinner. Both tales end in the suicide of the bereaved mistresses when they learn the identity of the excised hearts.[10] So obvious are the similarities between these two tales that we cannot help reconsidering the earlier one in light of this later version. The parallels between Tancredi's form of revenge and Guiglielmo's suggest that the prince is indeed acting more like a wronged husband than a scandalized father. This analogy is reinforced by the absence of any mention of Tancredi's wife, the notice of whose death we would expect in the opening passage of the story. Since an abundance of anagraphic information about the protagonists and their familial situations is the rule with Boccaccio, the lack of such information is important. Here the suppression of data about Tancredi's wife corresponds to the protagonist's own attitude, denying his past connubial state, as he denies that privilege to Ghismonda. The daughter thus becomes the recipient of Tancredi's unacknowledged drives, serving as surrogate for the wife whose name is never mentioned, and whose very existence is all but forgotten.

In his one-line response to Tancredi's accusation of adultery, Guiscardo articulates the theory of love which governs all three protagonists of the tale: "Amor può troppo più che né voi né io possiamo" (270). Boccaccio dignifies these words by making them the only ones which Guiscardo will utter in the entire tale. Syntactically and ideologically, this formula recalls Dante's damning commentary on courtly love which he placed in the mouth of Francesca da Rimini.[11]

---

[9] Auerbach does so, using this *anagnorisis* to illustrate his conviction that Boccaccian tragedy is the product of strictly gratuitous and arbitrary events. See *Mimesis*, pp. 230-231.

[10] In her structural analysis of the second *cuore-strappato* tale, Marga Cottino-Jones interprets the heart as a symbol richly endowed with cultural significance. See "The Mode and Structure of Tragedy in Boccaccio's *Decameron* (IV, 9)," *Italian Quarterly*, 11 (1967), 81.

[11] Russo claims that this Dantesque echo serves to distinguish Ghismonda's carnal passion from the more spiritualized love of Francesca for Paolo. See "Postilla critica a Ghismunda e Guiscardo," *Il Decameron*, p. 379. But these loves share more than Russo seems to suggest, for Francesca makes the body the exclusive subject of her lament. Phrases such as "costui de la bella persona" and "piacer sì forte" imply a physical desire so strong that its memory obsesses Francesca in an afterlife of eternal passion.

> Amor, ch'al cor gentil ratto s'apprende,
> prese costui de la bella persona
> che mi fu tolta; e 'l modo ancor m'offende.
> Amor, ch'a nullo amato amar perdona,
> mi prese del costui piacer sì forte,
> che, come vedi, ancor non m'abbandona.
> Amor condusse noi ad una morte.
>   (*Inf.* V, 100-106)

In this exposition of her amorous fall, Francesca reveals the metaphysic of courtly love. Her sin consists less in the adultery itself than in her abdication of moral responsibility for it—an abdication which the courtly love code invites. She displaces all responsibility for her adultery onto the abstract principle "Amor" which initiates each tercet and is the subject of almost all the active verbs within the passage. Paradoxically, the very passion which physically united Paolo and Francesca acts separately upon them in this explanation from beyond the grave. Love seizes first Paolo ("prese costui de la bella persona"), and only three lines later does it act upon Francesca, as she obeys the dictatorial command of "Amor, ch'a nullo amato amar perdona." Not until the last line are the lovers treated as a unit, when they share a single death ("una morte"). Despite Francesca's echo of Guinizelli in her opening line, this is anything but the gentle, suave love of the stilnovists. Dante's insertion of *ratto* in the Guinizellian line "al cor gentil ripara sempre Amore" and the subsequent word *prese* makes this passion a swift and predatory one. The stilnovists' theory of love as a potentiality residing within the gentle heart is utterly contradicted by Francesca's version of an external, dictatorial force which subjugates all lovers to its cruel whim.

When Guiscardo states simply "Amor può troppo più che né voi né io possiamo," he is invoking a similar concept of love. By including Tancredi in his statement ("né *voi* né io *possiamo*"), he articulates the truth that the reader has suspected all along: Tancredi's co-membership in this constituency of love.[12] What distinguishes the prince's subjugation from that of Ghismonda and Guiscardo is his unconsciousness—while the young paramours acknowledge their submission to the laws of courtly love, Tancredi does not.[13] Ironically, it is the holder of greatest political power who is most overpowered by the tyranny of love. And it is his denial of this superior force that makes Tancredi tyrannical in his own use of power, sabotaging his

---

[12] In *Vita di forme*, pp. 99-100, Getto concurs with Montale in calling this a love triangle.
[13] On the remarkable degree of unconsciousness which characterizes Tancredi's actions throughout the tale, see Baratto, pp. 181, 183.

performance of paternal and monarchal obligations. He fails as a father in his reluctance to give Ghismonda in marriage, while he fails as a ruler by not rewarding the superior service of Guiscardo. So Ghismonda takes her father to task for the undeserved poverty of her lover, "con tua vergogna si potrebbe concedere, ché così hai saputo un valente uomo tuo servidore mettere in buono stato" (273). Thus, it is not the adulterous love of Ghismonda and Guiscardo which is subversive of the social order, for the affair is carried out with a maximum of discretion, and would never have been discovered had not Tancredi so promiscuously violated his daughter's privacy. The truly subversive figure in the story is the prince himself, whose irresponsible and unconscious passion disqualifies him from any exercise of power.

Repression and denial are Tancredi's tragic flaws, undercutting the actions of an otherwise exemplary lord. But this theme has been treated in a polemic and then in a comic manner in the immediately preceding defense of Boccaccio's narrative mode. Indeed, the entire introduction to the fourth day, and the enclosed parable of Filippo Balducci, argue against the repression of amorous desires in literature.[14] We may suspect with some reason that Boccaccio is dramatizing in the tale of Tancredi the tragic consequences of the very sexual repression which his detractors are advocating in this polemic introduction to Day IV. In fact, three of the five charges which his critics level against the text concern its erotic content, when they complain that (1) Boccaccio likes women too much, (2) that he is beyond the age for love, and (3) that he should frequent the sphere of the Muses, not that of real women. Boccaccio answers his critics with a fiction in which he reveals the utter inadequacy of their suggestions for reform. The protagonist of the parable is Filippo Balducci, an elderly man who has renounced the joys of the world after the death of his wife. In Filippo, Boccaccio is enacting his critics' injunction to abandon women in his dotage. Filippo takes his young son with him to a mountaintop, actualizing Boccaccio's critics' suggestion that the writer repair to Mount Parnassus, and leave real women behind. Now Filippo's son is a frisky lad whose curiosity will not be satisfied by the sparse stimuli of a mountain retreat, so he begs his father to give him a glimpse of city life. Filippo agrees, feeling that his son must be well armed against the temptations of the flesh after eighteen years of religious exertion on a mountaintop, and introduces the boy to the wonders of Florence.

---

[14] Many critics read this tale as a manifesto of Boccaccio's naturalism. See, for example, Scaglione, *Nature and Love in the Late Middle Ages*, p. 105; R. Hastings, *Nature and Reason in the 'Decameron,'* p. 14; Baratto, p. 56. For the strange history of the tale of Filippo Balducci, once a misogynistic *exemplum* and now proof of the contrary, see Scaglione, pp. 102-105.

Much to the chagrin of Filippo, the boy is captivated by the sight of some young women returning from a wedding, and when he asks what they are called, the father tries to get his son off the track by labeling them *papere*. Through linguistic misrepresentation, Filippo thinks he can falsify the object of his son's desire, and thus extinguish the desire itself. But the lad cannot deny the evidence of his senses, despite Filippo's misnomer. The wise father acknowledges the failure of his expedient, and radically alters his linguistic approach to the problem of erotic desire. Since he cannot wish away his son's appetites, at least he can modify them by delivering a warning through metaphor. When Filippo answers his son's request for a pet goose with the objection "tu non sai donde elle s'imbeccano!" (264), the term *papere* has ceased to be a falsification for the reality of women and becomes instead a vehicle for a figurative teaching about female sexuality. Thus, Filippo's strategy of denial becomes one of disclosure through metaphor.

This tale, then, is less about a boy's sexual awakening than his father's lesson in fiction-making. Filippo learns that figurative language, far from masking its referent, can convey a truth with an efficacy superior to any equivalent literal expression. Indeed, Filippo's warning about female sexuality is far more pungent when expressed in terms of poultry than it would be if stated directly. That Boccaccio's interest in Filippo's example is linguistic may be proven by a comparison with earlier renditions of this same tale. In the *Novellino* version, a king must keep his son out of daylight for ten years, lest the child go blind. At the end of the appointed time, the boy is brought forth into the sun and allowed to see an array of beautiful things, among which are a sampling of women. When the child asks what these last are called, the king answers "dimoni." The boy's comment that he prefers the demons above all else causes the king to cry out in despair: "Che cosa tirannia è bellore di donna!"[15] In Boccaccio's version, not only are the *dimoni* replaced by *papere*, but the punch-line remains metaphorical, while the author of the *Novellino* concludes on a literal level. The later rendition replaces the misogynistic theme of the *Novellino* story with a lesson about the didactic possibilities of metaphor. Boccaccio further emphasizes the metalinguistic importance of the Balducci fable by using its teachings in his own defense. He answers his critics in metaphor by fictionalizing the policy of sexual repression which they would have him put into practice. The tale is metaphorical in the same way that the *papere* are—serving to illustrate the power of figurative language to illuminate, and not to mask, its counterpart in literal reality.

[15] *Novellino e conti del Duecento*, ed. Sebastiano Lo Nigro (Turin, 1968), p. 88.

The juxtaposition of Boccaccio's defense in the introduction to Day IV with the first of his tragic tales raises some problems of considerable interpretive importance. As mentioned before, the theme of sexual repression is present in both the Balducci parable and the tale of Tancredi.[16] Since the former is given a comic resolution by a certain manipulation of figurative language, we may expect that language will occupy a central position in the latter tale as well. A comparison of linguistic modes may lead us to some conclusions about what differentiates comic and tragic diction, and ultimately about the status of tragedy in the Boccaccian canon.

It is traditional for the lovers in tragedy to be the antagonists of social structure.[17] Their passion is seen as threatening to the survival and stability of an order which requires the containment of all energies in institutionalized forms. When the passion acquires the label of "courtly love" it becomes explicitly antisocial, for the code itself parodies and mocks the preeminent institutions of contemporary society: the Church, feudalism, and the judicial system.[18] Given, then, the built-in tension between courtly love and social structure, we might expect Boccaccio to set the adulterous couple squarely against the norms of the surrounding society. And he seems to be doing just that in the opposition of Ghismonda and Guiscardo to Tancredi, who, as prince of Salerno, is the spokesman for social structure within the tale. But this ostensible dichotomy is replaced by a more subtle and sinister one, for it is Tancredi himself, in his unconscious subjugation to the dictates of courtly love, who is in conflict with the norms of the society he is supposed to lead. Sabotaged by his own system of repression and denial, the prince violates all the distinctions upon which the social order depends: those between parent and child, male and female, lord and subject, aristocrat and commoner, elder and youth. The most fundamental of all oppositions, that of gender, suffers considerable damage at the hands of Tancredi. Father and daughter literally undergo a reversal of sex roles in their confrontation over the

[16] In "Symmetry and Balance in the *Decameron*," *Mediaevalia*, 2 (1976), 163-164, Janet Smarr notes the similarities between Filippo Balducci's and Tancredi's repressive approaches to their children's sexual interests.

[17] This conflict is well formulated by Northrop Frye. See *Anatomy of Criticism: Four Essays* (Princeton, 1973), p. 218.

[18] C.S. Lewis points out the parodic relationship between courtly love and the medieval Church in *The Allegory of Love* (New York, 1972), p. 18. The absorption of feudal terminology into the courtly-love code suggests the lovers' mimesis of that social system—with some significant inversions, such as the "lordship" of the lady (*midons*), the social disparity of knight and lady, etc. The medieval judicial system has its amorous equivalent in the courts of love and their attendant *questioni d'amore*. These last supply the format for some of the most famous pages of Boccaccio's early work, *Il Filocolo*.

discovered adultery,[19] when Ghismonda labels Tancredi "feminine" in his weakness and lacrimosity ("Or via, va con le femine a spander le lagrime" 273), while she herself overcomes any inclination to behave in the stereotyped way ascribed to her own sex. Although "dolore inestimabile sentì e a mostrarlo con romore e con lagrime, come il più le femine fanno, fu assai volte vicina" (271), nonetheless Ghismonda acts "non come dolente femina" (271) as her virile resolve takes precedence over any "womanly" tendency to tears. But this is not the first time that Ghismonda has acted according to our expectations of masculine behavior. In the conduct of her amorous intrigue she takes the traditional male role—a reversal necessitated by Tancredi's refusal to grant her the usual opportunities for matrimony.

Tancredi violates the distinctions between successive generations by failing to pass on to his juniors the privilege of marriage and procreation that he had enjoyed in his own time. He cannot differentiate between the demeanor proper to old age and youth, failing to exhibit the four attributes which Dante ascribes to the twilight years: prudence, justice, largesse, and affability.[20] In all of these, Tancredi proves wanting—so much so that he is reduced to a kind of senile infantilism, "piagnendo sì forte come farebbe un fanciul ben battuto" (271). Boccaccio sums up the incongruence of Tancredi's comportment to his years in the damning detail "ancora che vecchio fosse, da una finestra di quella si calò nel giardino" (270) as the prince escapes from his daughter's boudoir. Almansi suggests that this gesture is proof of the old man's sexual arousal, an observation which reinforces our own sense of the impropriety of such senescent behavior.

When Ghismonda defends her choice of a lover from the common ranks, Boccaccio reveals how Tancredi has violated yet another social distinction of paramount importance to the feudal order. Though Ghismonda's arguments are commonplaces of medieval thought, they nonetheless make explicit Tancredi's subversion of social hierarchy. Since nobility resides not in genealogy, but in the exercise of virtue, "colui che virtuosamente adopera, apertamente sé mostra gentile, e chi altramenti il chiama, non colui che è chiamato ma colui che chiama commette difetto" (272). This impersonal definition of gentility amounts to a scathing personal attack on Tancredi for his failure to discern and encourage virtue in his subordinates—a failure which places his own virtue in doubt. As king, his superior power to reward probity makes his negligence that much more reprehensible. Thus, Guiscardo, whose low birth is counteracted by his virtuous demeanor, and Tancredi, whose high rank is undercut by his delinquency, have

[19] On their exchange of attributes appropriate to each sex, see Baratto, p. 189.
[20] *Il Convivio*, trattato quarto, xxvii, 2.

exchanged places in the social hierarchy which theoretically puts virtue above genealogy.[21]

So wanton is Tancredi in his defiance of social distinctions that he breaches the most intimate of them all—that between the self and others. Thus, the prince persists in considering his daughter an extension of himself ("non sappiendola da sé partire") and disbelieves any evidence of her autonomy. When she promises to imitate the fate of Guiscardo should murder be his punishment, Tancredi cannot quite believe in the seriousness of her tragic resolve: "non credette per ciò in tutto lei sì fortemente disposta a quello che le parole sue sonavano" (273). Had he only believed her capable of such conviction, instead of assuming a false continuity between his will and her own, Tancredi would have heeded Ghismonda's suicidal threat and averted a double death. In his denial of Ghismonda's personal integrity and free will resides the most profound expression of Tancredi's tyranny, and the very source of his tragic fall.

Boccaccio links tyranny and tragedy in the frame story as well, making Tancredi's example paradigmatic of the impulse to tell tragic tales. When Filostrato ordains that Day IV be devoted to love stories which end unhappily ("si ragiona di coloro li cui amori ebbero infelice fine" 259), his rationale anticipates Tancredi's in its authoritarianism. It is significant, therefore, that Filostrato's "subjects" for the day, the other nine storytellers, seem to resent the imposition of a tragic theme for their narrations. We sense a note of reluctance in Fiammetta's prelude to her tale of Tancredi and Ghismonda, whose opening word "fiera" suggests the violence and bestiality which the *brigata* sought to escape in abandoning plague-ravaged Florence. "Fiera materia di ragionare n'ha oggi il nostro re data, pensando che, dove per rallegrarci venuti siamo, ci convenga raccontar l'altrui lagrime, le quali dir non si possono che chi le dice e chi l'ode non abbia compassione" (267). In the phrase "dove per rallegrarci venuti siamo," Fiammetta reveals how disparate Filostrato's purpose is from that of the rest of the storytelling *brigata*. When setting the ground rules for this pastoral sojourn, Pampinea had been emphatic about the exclusion of unpleasantness: "vogliamo e comandiamo che si guardi, dove che egli vada, onde che egli torni, che che egli oda o vegga, niuna novella altra che lieta ci rechi di fuori" (23-24). Pampinea dramatizes her purpose in the very phrasing of her command, using the circumlocution "altro che lieta" to replace any direct mention of unpleasantness. If the *Decameron* is to be one vast bulwark against bad news, why, then, generate disagreeable material from within its ordered confines?

---

[21] This paradox is observed by Almansi in *The Writer as Liar*, p. 148.

Since Pampinea is the authoress of this comic strategy, it is not surprising that she is the first to circumvent Filostrato's tragic theme. She does so without overtly breaking the law (for this is Dioneo's prerogative alone), sticking to the letter of Filostrato's ordinance while overlooking its spirit. Her saga of Frate Alberto (IV, 2) may end badly, but it is hardly one to arouse tears.[22] In choosing a humorous tale, Pampinea makes explicit the degree to which Filostrato has contravened the *brigata*'s will.

> Pampinea . . . più per la sua affezione cognobbe l'animo delle compagne che quello del re per le sue parole: e per ciò, più disposta a dovere alquanto recrear loro, che a dovere, fuori che del comandamento solo, il re contentare, a dire una novella, senza uscir del proposto, da ridere si dispose. (276)

It is Pampinea, then, who interprets for us "l'animo delle compagne" as one hostile to tragedy, and thus she feels no qualms about defying Filostrato, since his command is itself out of line—that is, it violates her own original injunction to levity. Pampinea's desire to "recrear" her colleagues is striking, and must be understood in its etymological sense of recreation,[23] for this indeed is Boccaccio's point in juxtaposing the storytelling enterprise with history at its most violent. The social order which has undergone such devastation in the throes of plague history is being recreated by this sojourn into fiction. It is no accident that a political model has been used to organize the storytelling activities according to a system of rotating rule—for this sets up a counter-example to the failing social order of the plague-stricken city. Harmony and consensus have typified the *brigata*'s government until now. Filostrato's imposition of an alien will on that of his constituents disrupts the smooth concord of this political experiment and brings into the pastoral retreat a tinge of the real world's unpleasantness.

But he makes amends. By telling the most amusing tale of Day V, Filostrato lends his full support to the restoration of a comic mood. That he offers the saga of the nightingale's song (V, 4) as atonement for the previous day's gloom is proved by his apologetic prelude to the tale. "Io sono stato da tante di voi tante volte morso perché io materia da crudeli ragionamenti e da farvi piagner v'imposi, che a me pare, a volere alquanto questa noia ristorare, esser tenuto di dover dire alcuna cosa per la quale io alquanto vi faccia ridere" (356). To seal his atonement, Filostrato makes his present narration a corrective to the

---

[22] Marga Cottino-Jones finds in this comic tale a stabilizing force which gives Day IV a poetic balance. See *An Anatomy of Boccaccio's Style*, p. 97.

[23] "Ricreare: creare di nuovo . . . [dal lat. recreare]," in Giacomo Devoto, Gian Carlo Oli, *Dizionario della lingua italiana* (Florence, 1971), p. 1941.

keynote tale of Day IV—that of Tancredi and Ghismonda.[24] The story of Ricciardo Manardi and Caterina undoes the tragic action of this earlier plot, proving that the crisis which precipitates Ghismonda's suicide is not the result of inexorable fate, and in fact need not have occurred at all. The two tales share a similar set of preconditions. Caterina, like Ghismonda, is an over-protected daughter who has reached a marriageable age and is impatient to experience the joys of the flesh. Like Ghismonda, she arranges a clandestine meeting with her lover, and like her counterpart in the earlier tale, is caught *in flagrante*. But the denouements of these two plots are as different as the genres of comedy and tragedy themselves, for one ends in a double death, as the younger generation precedes its elder into the grave, while the other ends in marriage and assimilation into the social structure as power is gracefully transmitted from one generation to the next. Of course, the psychosexual dynamic of the second tale is benign from the start, and a close look at it will reveal more differences than similarities between the family situations of Caterina and Ghismonda. Though Caterina is also an only child born in her father's dotage, the active presence of the mother in the story defuses the incestuous possibilities which govern Ghismonda's fate. The suitors in each story have enjoyed positions of some trust in the fathers' households: Guiscardo as a servant brought up from early childhood under the auspices of the prince, and Ricciardo as a friend whose comings and goings are as free as any son's would be, "del quale niuna altra guardia messer Lizio o la sua donna prendevano che fatto avrebbon d'un lor figliuolo" (357). The crises of both tales are accompanied by linguistic manipulations which merit special attention if we are to discover that certain use of language which is the touchstone of tragedy in Boccaccio.

The saga of Ricciardo and Caterina may be read as an adventure in circumlocuation. Throughout the tale, these young people seek a hidden language of love—one which will figuratively express their desire and facilitate its fulfillment, without exciting the suspicions of over-protective parents. The first exchange between Ricciardo and Caterina is indeed figurative, though so commonplace that it could hardly succeed in concealing their passion from prying eyes. "'Caterina, io ti priego che tu non mi facci morire amando.' La giovane rispose subito: 'Volesse Idio che tu non facessi più morir me!'" (357). By responding to Ricciardo's figurative appeal in kind, Caterina signals not only her reciprocity but her cooperation in his quest for a

---

[24] The link between this tale and that of the nightingale has been observed by Stavros Deligiorgis in *Narrative Intellection in the 'Decameron,'* p. 114, and Janet Smarr in "Symmetry and Balance," p. 164.

figurative language of love. The first metaphor which Caterina puts to such service is that of amorous "heat." Thus, she complains of the stifling nights which keep her awake with "lo soperchio caldo" (357). When her mother disagrees with Caterina's perception of the weather, the girl must make her metaphor more explicit yet. "Voi dovreste pensare quanto sieno più calde le fanciulle che le donne attempate" (358). Caterina has almost let her literal meaning slip through this thin veil of figurative language. The term *fanciulle* with its connotations of maidenhood[25] suggests the sexual tenor of this nearly transparent vehicle. Seeing the success of such a strategy on her mother, whose solicitousness for her daughter's comfort surpasses her parental vigilance, the girl invents the metaphor which will allow her finally to enjoy Ricciardo's embraces. Caterina consequently argues that a bed on the veranda will not only help her survive the summer heat, but will also permit her to hear the nightingale's song. Though her skeptical father seems to question the sincerity of Caterina's interest in birds ("che rusignuolo è questo a che ella vuol dormire?" 358), he is nonetheless convinced by the importunings of his wife that "i giovani son vaghi delle cose simiglianti a loro" (358) and that he therefore should not marvel "perché egli le sia in piacere l'udir cantar l'usignuolo" (358). When Lizio finally grants his daughter's request to sleep on the veranda, answering, "dormavi e oda cantar l'usignuolo a suo senno" (358), he is unwittingly sanctioning the literal activity of lovemaking which this metaphor conceals.[26]

Caterina's night on the veranda does little to alleviate the problem of overheating, for the lovers remain "sì ancora riscaldati sì dal tempo e sì dallo scherzare, senza alcuna cosa adosso s'adormentarono" (359). But she apparently does satisfy her longing for the nightingale's song, "molte volte faccendo cantar l'usignuolo" (359). When Lizio awakens the next morning to behold the success of his daughter's night *al fresco*, he discovers the literal meaning of the nightingale metaphor and invites his wife to share the revelation: "Vieni a vedere che tua figliuola è stata sì vaga dell'usignuolo che ella l'ha preso e tienlosi in mano" (359).

The crisis is not so much this graphic discovery as Lizio's decision about what course of justice to take. At a similar juncture in another

[25] "Fanciulla: per estens. giovane che ha superato la pubertà, ragazza adulta o da marito, giovane donna (sposata o vedova, donna nubile di qualsiasi età)," *Grande dizionario della lingua italiana*, V, ed. Salvatore Battaglia (Turin, 1968), 631.

[26] For a thorough analysis of the metaphoric uses and abuses of nightingales in this story, see Cesare Segre, "Da Boccaccio a Lope de Vega," *Boccaccio: Secoli di vita, Atti del Congresso Internazionale, Boccaccio, 1975*, ed. Marga Cottino-Jones and Edward F. Tuttle (Ravenna, 1977), pp. 234-235.

story, Tancredi opted for tragedy by plotting a revenge as dark and secret as the lovers' intrigue had been. But Lizio opts for comedy by instantaneously granting Caterina and Ricciardo the chance to enjoy such evenings on a permanent basis, thus signaling his willingness to transmit power from the old generation to the new—a process which Tancredi could not bring himself to accept. That Lizio sanctions the legitimacy of the young people's desires is proved by his very complicity in their language of love. He consciously accepts his daughter's metaphoric system by continuing to speak of the sexual act in nightingale terms even after he discovers the true meaning of the circumlocution. Lizio executes a brilliant linguistic maneuver for accommodating the lovers' passion to the demands of bourgeois respectability by making their metaphor of fornication into a conceit of marriage.[27] With the introduction of "la gabbia" into the lovers' figurative system, Lizio has found a witty way to extend the nightingale's one-night stand into a permanent sojourn, "sì che egli si troverà aver messo l'usignuolo nella gabbia sua e non nell'altrui" (360).[28] Of course, Boccaccio cannot resist one final ambiguity, when he consigns his couple to an indefinite future of bird-catching, in which Ricciardo, together with Caterina, "lungamente in pace e in consolazione uccellò agli usignuoli e di dì e di notte quanto gli piacque" (361). The touch of malice in this verb "uccellò," however, is only enough to add to the general merriment of this comic resolution.

At the critical moment when Lizio chooses to have mercy on the wayward lovers, he so signals by entering into their system of metaphoric discourse. Since Tancredi's justice takes the opposite course from that of Lizio's, we may expect that his language will move away from metaphor to the level of literality. And this is indeed the case, for Tancredi's punishment is accompanied by a linguistic transgression as shocking as the revenge itself. When the prince sends his daughter the token of her lover's excised heart, he has literalized the central metaphor of courtly love. What tradition had deemed the locus of the most intangible and ethereal human virtues, Tancredi reduces to a mass of bleeding tissue. Ghismonda makes explicit the linguistic nature of Tancredi's trespass as she mourns the sacrificial heart. "Ahi! dolcissimo albergo di tutti i miei piaceri, maladetta sia la crudeltà di colui che con gli occhi della fronte or mi ti fa vedere! Assai

[27] In Lizio's spontaneous artistry, as he accommodates the lover's situation to his own standards of bourgeois respectability, B.J. Layman sees another of the internal artist figures with which Boccaccio punctuates his text. See "Boccaccio's Paradigm of the Artist and His Art," *Italian Quarterly*, 13 (Winter 1970), 31-32.

[28] Šklovsky takes the figure one step further, identifying Ricciardo with the nightingale who is caught and caged. "Egli stesso si è trasformato in una metafora." See *La lettura del 'Decameron,'* p. 217.

m'era con quegli della mente riguardarti a ciascuna ora" (274). In this poignant lament, Ghismonda reveals the vast difference between her own refined sensibility and her father's reductive rage. By making Guiscardo's heart visible to "gli occhi della fronte," Tancredi has restored the metaphor to its origins in human physiology. Almansi notes that the prince, like Guiglielmo Rossiglione (IV, 9), sees the heart in exclusively physical terms, "as pre-eminently an organ to be torn out and away."[29] Operating on the assumption that his daughter's love is of a purely carnal sort, the prince presupposes that the extinction of Guiscardo's body will extinguish the passion as well, and thus "pensò con gli altrui danni raffreddare il suo fervente amore" (273). But Ghismonda proves that her love transcends mere concupiscence by restoring a metaphoric dimension to the lover's heart which Tancredi has placed before her eyes. Ghismonda's language reverses the reductive movement of Tancredi's when she assigns to this anatomical part "the resting place of love in all its manifestations whether physical or spiritual."[30] In the order of her discourse, Ghismonda gives primacy to the metaphoric interpretation of this *topos*, as she inverts the temporal sequence of events, lamenting first the accessibility of Guiscardo's heart to "gli occhi della fronte" and returning to the season when it was visible only to "quegli della mente." This movement back in time fittingly ends with the figurative attribution of eyes to the mind, making the distinction between "then" and "now"—between the past of amorous bliss and the present of cruel revenge—the distinction between metaphoric and literal truth. Looking back over the earlier course of Ghismonda's passion, when she and Guiscardo enjoy their amorous embraces, we see that the conduct of their affair is governed by metaphor. In the very mode of conveyance by which Ghismonda chooses to send Guiscardo a first message, she figures the ensuing acts of love. The message is given to Guiscardo with the instructions: "fara'ne questa sera un soffione alla tua servente, col quale ella raccenda il fuoco" (268). Topographically, the hillside which conceals a tunnel under its surface growth of thorns and brambles is a metaphor of female anatomy. And of course, Guiscardo's forays into this secret conduit, when he is sheathed in leather, anticipates the physiology of the activities to follow.[31] Through such figurative devices, the lovers are able to conduct their affair "discretamente" using neutral signs to facilitate their liaison, and hiding their passion from those who may be hurt or scandalized by it.

And so the affair might have continued indefinitely, nourished by

[29] Almansi, *The Writer as Liar*, p. 150.
[30] Ibid.
[31] Ibid., p. 141.

metaphor, had not Tancredi violated first the privacy of his daughter's bedchamber, and then the terms of metaphor itself by presenting Guiscardo's heart to "gli occhi della fronte." The presentation speech which accompanies Tancredi's gift to Ghismonda reveals the contorted logic of revenge. The message is uttered by "un suo segretissimo famigliare" (273) whose intercession renders Tancredi's message that much more twisted and indirect. "Il tuo padre ti manda questo per consolarti di quella cosa che tu più ami, come tu hai lui consolato di ciò che egli più amava" (273). The density of personal pronouns, many of which are grammatically unnecessary, heightens the accusatory tone of this message. In the multiplicity of second person and third person singular forms (*tuo, ti, ti, tu, tu, lui, egli*), Tancredi recapitulates the drama of filial love and betrayal which he has obviously relived time and again in his vengeful fantasy. But it is in the choice of verbs, and in the refusal to name "quella cosa" and "ciò che," that Tancredi reveals his true psychology. Incapable of his daughter's metaphoric understanding which can discern hidden truths in concrete objects, Tancredi can only make sarcastic substitutions of words with their opposites. Thus, "consolation" really means "punishment" as the prince sends Ghismonda the heart of her lover to "console" (read "punish") Ghismonda's "consolatory" (read "punitive") behavior toward her father. Tancredi's reluctance to specify "quella cosa" and "ciò che" indicates less discretion than cowardice, as does his decision to have a third person deliver the message rather than face Ghismonda himself.

But the great irony of this passage is that, when read metaphorically, it contains the elements of a comic resolution. If Tancredi had really wanted to "console" his daughter, he could have done precisely that by giving her Guiscardo's heart figuratively in marriage. Then the chain of consolations would be complete, each link being forged in the appropriate season: as Ghismonda had consoled her father with filial love, so she would be consoled by the love of a husband in the prime of her life. But only in death is such a resolution possible, as the lovers are finally allowed to lie together, and their love is made public according to Ghismonda's last wish. Only now is the proper order of the family restored, as the triangle of love, in which Ghismonda had stood at the apex of both men's desires, is finally righted and Tancredi gains ascendency over the couple in his capacity as father and king.

With a tardiness which has characterized his relations to Ghismonda throughout the tale (late in arranging her marriage, late in acknowledging her tragic resolve) Tancredi atones for his cruelty by granting his daughter's final request. "Dopo molto pianto e tardi pentuto della sua crudeltà, con general dolore di tutti i salernetani,

onorevolmente amenduni in un medesimo sepolcro gli fé sepellire"
(275).

In this concluding passage, the action moves beyond the castle walls
and embraces the entire population of Salerno. Such an opening up
of the plot is striking in a tale which has hitherto confined itself to the
inner recesses of a castle, and to the secret intrigue of three characters. The tragic action thus produces a kind of ripple effect, radiating
outward in ever larger concentric circles of influence. Already within
the castle walls a miniature public has borne witness to the last mo-
ments of Ghismonda's life as the ladies-in-waiting behold the torren-
tial tears, the farewell speech, and the self-inflicted death of their
mistress. Tancredi's extension of the resolution to include all of
Salerno has reverberations which reach beyond the confines of the
tale itself. For now the members of the frame story *brigata* follow the
model of the two internal publics in sorrow. "Aveva la novella dalla
Fiammetta raccontata le lagrime più volte tirate infino in su gli occhi
alle sue compagne" (276). By extrapolation, we the readers would
constitute the fourth concentric circle in this succession of grieving
publics.

The final note of this tragedy, then, is a unifying one. Not only are
four distinct publics brought together in common grief, but Tancredi
is himself restored to harmony with his subjects by resuming his proper place as ruler of Salerno. This restoration of order is what Northrop Frye terms "nemesis," that is, the "righting of the balance"[32]
which the tragic hero has disturbed. Not only is a political and
psychological equilibrium established, but a narrative one as well, for
the ending of the tale completes the tragic circle anticipated in the
opening passages, where Boccaccio intimated that Tancredi's record
as "signore assai umano e di benigno ingegno" would be stained by
"amoroso sangue." Now the deed is done, our expectations fulfilled,
and order brought to the grieving citizens of Salerno. But a certain
uneasiness mars our aesthetic satisfaction with this plot, not only because tragedy is itself inimicable to the prevailing mood of the text,
but because this resolution bears too close a resemblance to comedy,
and in so doing reminds us of the happier ending in which the couple
is allowed to marry, the social order is renewed, and the entire community united in joy.[33] Here, instead, the couple shares not marriage
bonds, but a common death, the society remains under the old order,
and unity is achieved in grief.[34]

---

[32] Frye, *An Anatomy of Criticism*, p. 209.
[33] See Frye's formula for comic resolution, on his p. 163.
[34] The relationship between comedy and tragedy is a highly debated one. In Frye's
theory that all genres derive from an archetypal quest myth, comedy contains tragedy

Boccaccio need not tell us where his own preferences lie—his storytelling *brigata* does that for him. Once Filostrato is soundly scolded for his tragic tastes, the storytellers return to comedy with renewed wit and resolve. Perhaps Day IV is necessary to purge the *brigata* of any vestigial tendencies to tragedy, and perhaps these tales perform a valuable service in exorcizing such demons from the tellers' imaginations, as well as from our own.

It is here that I join Branca in refuting Auerbach's judgment of Boccaccio's tragic style.[35] On the grounds that he is sentimental and unsure in handling tragedy, Auerbach wants to banish Boccaccio from the heights of tragic discourse, for this is when "the vagueness and uncertainty of his early humanism becomes apparent. His realism . . . becomes weak and superficial as soon as the problematic or the tragic is touched upon."[36] Here again, this critic who is otherwise so superb in matters of genre and style ignores Boccaccio's subtle use of narrative form. Auerbach fails to place Boccaccio's tales in the contextual whole which determines our reading of its individual parts. The fact that the tragic tales constitute an "aberration" in the text, that the storytellers continually lament the injunction to tell tragic tales, and that other stories in subsequent days virtually undercut the tragic necessity of Day IV's narration, suggest that Boccaccio is making contextual commentaries on the inadequacy of tragedy as a literary mode.[37] When Auerbach bemoans Boccaccio's fetishistic attachment to physical objects, like the excised hearts, he misses the writer's own indictment of tragic language as literal-minded. By failing to compare the literalization of metaphor which results in excised hearts to those comic tales which make metaphors out of real things, the critic overlooks Boccaccio's entire polemic about the linguistic constituents of tragedy. Through the isolation of tragic diction in Day IV, Boccaccio reveals by contrast the linguistic mode which will govern the rest of

(*Anatomy of Criticism*, p. 215). In reviewing René Girard's *La violence et le sacré*, in which tragedy is seen as the ur-mode, Robert J. Nelson shows how Plato's *Symposium* casts doubt on Girard's thesis. Taking Girard's argument one step further (or back), Nelson entertains the possibility that comedy may even be the anterior mode, positing a time of primal peace and coherence before the "sacred state of violence" (48). See "Ritual Reality, Tragic Imitation, Mythic Projection," *Diacritics*, 6 (Summer 1976), 41-48.

[35] See Branca, *Boccaccio medievale*, p. 28.

[36] Auerbach, p. 231.

[37] For another, very different reading of Boccaccio's tragedy, see Vittorio Russo, "Il senso del tragico nel *Decameron*," *Filologia e letteratura*, 11 (1965), 29-83. Russo reads the tragic tales as central to Boccaccio's dialectic of fortune and human will, illustrating one of man's two possible responses to the power of fortune in worldly affairs. See his p. 53. Russo traces Boccaccian tragedy back to Senecan theater, and sees it as the forerunner of Renaissance tragic drama.

the text. Henceforth, the language of the *Decameron* will be that of nightingales, *papere*, and devils in Hell—not that of hearts which bleed real blood.

IV

BOCCACCIO'S SINGULAR CICERO

THE TALE OF FRATE CIPOLLA (VI, 10)

—Study of linguistic relativism (69)
— onion as metaphor for duplicity (76)

When he is at his most humorous and irreverent, Boccaccio delivers perhaps his gravest commentaries on the status of fiction within the human order. The relationships between sign and meaning, between figurative and literal, between narrative and fact are scrupulously examined in these tales whose sole apparent purpose is to entertain. The surface fun hides the more sinister implications of Boccaccio's wit which casts doubt on his culture's basic assumptions about literary creation. For Boccaccio, human utterance is no longer a vehicle for divine teachings, and providential discourse becomes instead a presumptuous, dangerous claim to embody a transcendent truth which resists human formulation. Boccaccio's stories reveal the unstable, fluctuating, and deceptive quality of literary constructs by exposing the equivocal uses to which they are put, and the self-serving beneficiaries of fictive creation. The tale of Frate Cipolla is such a story, and it invites the reader's closest critical attention as a metaliterary statement of signal importance.

Guido Almansi alerts us to a "system of signposting"[1] whereby the author leads his reader to the ideological core of his work. One of these signposts, suggests Almansi, is the location of a passage within the structure of the whole. By such standards, the tale of Frate Cipolla gains prominence as the culmination of a crucial storytelling day, itself physically central to the text. The theme of Day VI, "nella quale, sotto il reggimento d'Elissa, si ragiona di chi con alcun leggiadro motto, tentato, si riscotesse, o con pronta risposta o avvedimento fuggì perdita o pericolo o scorno" (403), is a concise formulation of the very

---

[1] Almansi, *The Writer as Liar*, p. 19.

logic of the frame story itself. By asserting the power of words to modify a hostile situation, Day VI reflects the organizing principle of the entire *Decameron* whose storytellers are responding to historical adversity (the plague) with a verbal counter-creation (the tales). This synecdochic relationship between Day VI and the text lends special dignity and weight to its ten stories of rescue by repartee. Of the last tale in Day VI, we may therefore entertain great hopes, expecting to find in it a decisive formulation of narrative intent, an assertion of verbal efficacy, a revelation of Boccaccio's poetics at its most brilliant. These hopes are perversely fulfilled by Fra Cipolla and his servant Guccio Imbratta, variously called Guccio Porco or Guccio Balena, whose multiple names are central to the theory of language advanced in this tale.

Cipolla is a mendicant friar who travels about the countryside for alms and nearly meets with disaster in the provincial town of Certaldo. He promises his congregation the spectacle of a wing-feather from the Angel Gabriel in return for contributions to the protective society of Sant'Antonio. Two local pranksters plan to sabotage the performance by exchanging the feather for a lump of coal—a program which is easily executed since Guccio, who is supposed to be guarding the relic, is downstairs in the hotel kitchen wooing the scullery-maid Nuta. Cipolla does not discover the exchange until mid-sermon, when he has already exquisitely prepared his parishioners for the angelic relic. Undaunted, he takes his listeners on an imaginary pilgrimage to the Holy Land, where he discovers a store of the most unthinkable sacred objects, including the coals of the martyred San Lorenzo. So fantastic is his travelogue and his sacred inventory that the revelation of the coals seems not only tenable, but anticlimactic. The crowd's gullibility goads Cipolla into two final inventions: a year's worth of fire insurance for those whose doublets are marked with a cross by San Lorenzo's coals, and the miraculous regrowth of the coals equal to the volume lost in marking the doublets. At the conclusion of this performance, the two pranksters reveal their trick to Cipolla and return the feather which the friar then employs the following year with equal success.

Another way in which Boccaccio singles out Frate Cipolla for special attention is by a series of allusions to other tales throughout the text. The story looks backwards and forwards with Janus-like intelligence, subsuming the six days of the preceding narration and anticipating the four to come. The freshest recall is to the unsightly Baronci of VI, 6 to whom Guccio's beloved Nuta is compared. Other echoes of tales past include the Angel Gabriel of IV, 2 and the nightingale of V, 4 who makes a metaphoric appearance in this story when Guccio finds himself more comfortable in Nuta's kitchen than "sopra i verdi rami l'usignuolo" (431). The name Guccio Imbratta also occurs in IV, 7 referring to one of the four undertakers whose grisly job it is to bury the swollen bodies of La Simona and Pasquino.

Frate Cipolla looks ahead to an entire subgenre of stories that will typify the later days of the *Decameron*. These are tales of the *beffatori* and *buffoni*, of the *furbi* and the *fessi* whose pranks are so dear to the Florentine fancy. Cipolla's allusion to Maso del Saggio, the nutshell salesman whom he allegedly meets in his odyssey to the Holy Land, foreshadows the Calandrino series of VIII, 3 and 6 and IX, 3 and 5. Maso really initiates the whole chain of practical jokes which constitute this subgenre by inspiring Calandrino's unfortunate quest for the heliotrope in VIII, 3. In a later tale (VIII, 5) Maso will occupy center stage along with two other pranksters who remove the breeches of a judge from the Marches.

By incorporating so many allusions to other tales in this story, Boccaccio makes of it a way station in the course of his text. Frate Cipolla's example gives the author an excuse to stand back and contemplate the progress of his work, to assess retrospectively his achievement and to anticipate its future direction. Not surprisingly, Boccaccio has chosen as his vehicle a story about a storyteller whose verbal escapades recall an earlier tale of considerable metaliterary importance. That is the tale of Ser Ciappelletto in which Boccaccio introduces the principles governing his narrative world. The tale of Frate Cipolla is surely its companion piece—together they constitute a revelation of the storyteller's art at its most powerful and perverse. The similarities between the names Ciappelletto and Cipolla should be enough to raise the reader's suspicions at the outset. Both include virtuoso liars in the role of storyteller, both internalize the public dimension of the genre, both expose the mechanisms of narrative seduction.[2] But there is a radical change in emphasis in the latter tale. Whereas the example of Ser Ciappelletto generated a moralizing gloss which twisted the protagonist's mischief into perverse proof of divine benevolence, Cipolla's tale necessitates no exegesis. In the six days of storytelling which intervene between Ser Ciappelletto and Frate Cipolla, the frame story narrators have dispensed with the impulse to read providential significance into human fiction. They no longer feel the need to justify their artifacts in the name of an external system of meaning, and can now accept the absolute autonomy of their fictional construct.

---

[2] Mazzotta comments on the complementarity of these two tales in "The Marginality of Literature," p. 73, while Marga Cottino-Jones, in "Magic and Superstition," p. 10, sees in both protagonists the ability to exploit the religious superstitions of their parishioners.

The fact that Cipolla's falsifications occasion no moralizing gloss, as Ciappelletto's had, indicates the great distance Boccaccio has traveled in freeing his fictions from any obligations to interpretive systems beyond the text.

Another signpost of Cipolla's importance is the juxtaposition of this story with the noble and mysterious tale of Guido Cavalcanti (VI, 9). The latter contains perhaps the most serious and disturbing statement of the artist's relationship to social structure and to its ideological suppositions in the entire text. The tale records a test between the philosopher-artist Guido and the members of Betto Brunelleschi's *brigata* which Guido refuses to join. As one critic put it, "their differences from Cavalcanti are profound: they are aggressive, jocular, gregarious, and one is either with them or against them."[3] A dichotomy is present from the very start of the tale in the characterization of these rival factions. Conformity and anonymity typify the *brigata* which functions as an undifferentiated whole in all its operations. The adverbial *insieme* punctuates all descriptions of its collective acts: "si ragunavano insieme i gentili uomini delle contrade . . . similmente si vestivano insieme almeno una volta l'anno, e insieme i dì più notabili cavalcavano per la città" (426). So strong is this tendency to conformity that it reduces Boccaccio's prose to the formulaic sameness of imperfect verbs with generic or impersonal subjects. Guido, on the other hand, keeps quite to himself, for the very gifts which would most adorn him in polite company—eloquence and gentle manners—are precisely those which elevate him beyond the pale of normal social activity. "Ogni cosa che far volle e a gentile uom pertenente seppe *meglio che altro uom fare* [emphasis mine]" (427).

Perhaps the greatest cause for Guido's alienation is his allegiance to the thought of Epicurus ("egli alquanto tenea della oppinione degli epicuri" (427). This heresy renders him "abstratto dagli uomini" (427) in a double sense: by virtue of the philosophical activity itself, which removes him from the daily concourse of men, and by virtue of the specific philosophy of Guido's choice. His Epicurean rejection of the soul's immortality would necessarily distance him from the society whose entire moral system depends on an afterlife of reward and punishment.

The dialectic between solitude and solidarity is never really resolved, though Guido does end the tug-of-war by shaming the *brigata* into an awareness of its limited perspective. When he calls out from among the tombstones of Santa Reparata, "Signori, voi mi potete dire a casa vostra ciò che vi piace" (427), he bursts the convivial bubble of

[3] Deligiorgis, *Narrative Intellection*, p. 146.

the revelers by reminding them of their common end.[4] It is Betto, the self-appointed exegete of Guido's remark, who interprets "casa vostra" as the tombs in the cemetery, and explains to his men that they are "peggio che uomini morti" (428). By including this gloss within the tale, Boccaccio reveals the success of Guido's edifying repartee, and demonstrates its effects on a public whose awareness of its common assumptions is surely raised. As a result, Betto's men finally cease bothering Guido, and accord him the dignity of his solitude. There emerges from this tale the portrait of the artist as a disinterested custodian of social consciousness who remains estranged from his community in order to judge it. He refuses to humor his public by reinforcing its illusions of privilege and permanence, but takes it to task instead for the sin of complacency. He is by necessity alone, unable to brook the moral compromises built into the society of men.

It is easy to see in this story a respectful Boccaccio, inspired by the nobility of Guido, and eager to emulate his example. The sharp-tongued poet who transcends public opinion while he moulds it, dramatizes an artistic ideal to which Boccaccio strives throughout his apologetics. We may wonder, then, why the writer decides to juxtapose this exemplary figure of the artist with a reprehensible one by following the tale of Guido Cavalcanti with that of Frate Cipolla. We look in vain for any consistency in Boccaccio's textual embodiments of his narrative role, unless we choose to see Cipolla as a storyteller *in malo* whose language determines, by contrast, Boccaccio's own. Whereas the tale of Guido directly asserts the edifying power of words, that of Frate Cipolla does so indirectly, by allowing Boccaccio's voice to triumph where his protagonist's fails. Though the characterizations of Guido and Cipolla are diametrically opposed, their commentaries on storytelling are therefore of a piece.[5]

Among the first things that we learn about this mendicant friar of Sant'Antonio is that he thrives on company. His network of friendships extends throughout Certaldo, "quasi di tutti quegli della contrada era compare o amico o benvogliente" (430), making him "il miglior brigante del mondo" (429-430). Cipolla's intimacy with his public has, of course, serious implications for his storytelling mode. Whereas Guido stands aloof and challenges the norms of his society in the name of philosophical truth, Cipolla remains within the commun-

---

[4] Šklovsky sees in Guido's comment the distinction between the cultural conservatism of society at large and the solitary humanism of those who pursue their "nuova scienza." See *La lettura del 'Decameron,'* p. 213.

[5] In Getto's analysis, the juxtaposition of these tales is a classist study in intelligence, with Guido representing an aristocratic intellectual ideal, and Cipolla a plebian one. See *Vita di forme*, p. 159.

ity and exploits its biases to his personal advantage. Neither we nor Boccaccio, however, judge him ill for such flagrant mismanagement of language, since his consenting public neutralizes any indictments of fraudulent bad faith on the part of the friar. The Certaldans fully subscribe to Cipolla's methodology, offering the quintessential examples of what Luigi Russo calls "il mondo che vuole essere ingannato."[6]

Language, for Cipolla, becomes a pliant instrument of expedient, submissive to the needs of his public and to his own mercenary ends. His rhetoric bespeaks no absolute system of meaning, but remains fluid and unstable in the service of a lucrative profession. The entire tale becomes a study of linguistic relativism, of its genesis and uses in the self-serving world of Cipolla and his variously named servant. For the protagonists, words are no longer signs pointing to extralinguistic significance, but elements in a system which is entirely self-referential. Yet before Cipolla can reconstitute a new language obedient to its own laws of signification, he must destroy the old one. This he accomplishes by emptying language of all conventional content and disabusing his public of any linguistic preconceptions it may bring to his discourse. At the end of his sermon, when Cipolla must explain to the congregation the absence of the feather and the presence of the coals, his verbal technique borders on the nonsensical. To quote Russo, "direi che il discorso di fra Cipolla diventa come insensato, senza alcuna corrispondenza di fatti o di nomi egli si accontenta di ammassare parole su parole."[7] But we have suspected Cipolla of pure bombast from the very beginning. Boccaccio describes the friar's oratorical skills with damning praise: "niuna scienza avendo, sì ottimo parlatore e pronto era, che chi conosciuto non l'avesse, non solamente un gran rettorico l'avrebbe estimato, ma avrebbe detto esser Tulio medesimo o forse Quintiliano" (430). In this telling passage, Boccaccio offers a crisscross of panegyric and reproach. The main clauses celebrate Cipolla's rhetorical prowess, while the subordinate clauses expose the ignorance at its core. If we read every second phrase, we get an unadulterated portrait of excellence—one which the intervening clauses totally invalidate. This passage typifies the ambivalence which Boccaccio will manifest toward his singular Cicero throughout the tale.

The most damning observation of all is Boccaccio's initial one: "niuna scienza avendo," implying that Cipolla's surface brilliance hides deep chasms of ignorance, that his rhetoric is an insubstantial

[6] Russo, *Il Decameron*, p. 428.
[7] Ibid., p. 441.

confection of pure style.[8] The friar's art may thus be labeled sophistic in its emphasis on virtuosity and its indifference to content. His techniques of dilation and improvisation indeed suggest "what must become of rhetoric without the urgencies of matter and motive."[9]

It is not by accident that Cipolla's original relic, the feather of the Angel Gabriel, should come from a parrot. Cesare Ripa's collection of *Iconologia* includes this bird in the emblem for eloquence, perched on top of an open cage at the foot of a lady dressed in red. The parrot signifies an aspect of eloquence which is key to this study: the speaker's ability to orate on any topic without background expertise. "Il papagallo è simbolo dell'eloquente perchè si rende maraviglioso colla lingua e con le parole, imitando l'huomo, nella cui lingua solamente consiste l'essercitio dell'eloquenza."[10] The bird's mimesis of human discourse is a purely mechanical act, a movement of the tongue which produces humanoid sounds. Like the parrot, Cipolla has the vocal apparatus of the orator, but not the prerequisite knowledge.

In the three groups of rhymed triads which Cipolla uses to describe his benighted servant Guccio, Boccaccio offers a striking example of the friar's reduction of language to pure sound.[11] "Egli è tardo, sugliardo e bugiardo; negligente, disubidente e maldicente; trascutato, smemorato e scostumato" (431). So enchanting is this virtuoso performance in rhymed prose that we forget to consider its meaning. It is as if we were placed in an echo chamber where sounds are endlessly replicated—we admire the gimmick, but do not ask what meaning it conveys. Later in his sermon, Cipolla will use this technique again when he invents the locales of "Truffia" and "Buffia," jabberwocky combinations of *trucco* and *beffa* which ricochet off each other like *abracadabra*.

The polynomasia of Guccio Imbratta, alias Porco, alias Balena, offers a case study in Cipollan linguistics.[12] If one man can have three

---

[8] In this, Cipolla breaks the medieval rhetorician's Golden Rule. Goeffrey of Vinsauf warns that stylistic virtuosity is worthless unless endowed with an interior meaning which completes its exterior charm. See Edmond Faral, *Les arts poétiques du XIIe et du XIIIe siècle* (Paris, 1924), pp. 284-285.

[9] Charles Sears Baldwin, *Medieval Rhetoric and Poetic* (New York, 1928), p. 12.

[10] Cesare Ripa, *Iconologia* (Padua, 1611), p. 139.

[11] In *Boccaccio medievale*, p. 57, Branca sees this tripling as a parody of the linguistic lessons taught by Isidore of Seville. On Boccaccio's patterns of three linked adjectives in this tale, and elsewhere (*Dec.* VI, 8), see Franco Fido, "Boccaccio's *Ars Narrandi* in the Sixth Day of the *Decameron*," pp. 232-233.

[12] We might note in passing the relevance of Guccio's multiple surnames to the various contexts in which he appears. When he is ensconced in Nuta's filthy kitchen, he is called Imbratta, from the verb *imbrattare*—to soil. The surname Porco obtains when the two pranksters eye him wooing Nuta. We learn from Cesare Ripa's *Iconologia* that the pig is the symbol of debauchery (p. 112), gluttony (p. 209), and lethargy (p. 397).

different names, then the bond between a unitary sign and a unitary meaning has been broken, and in the absence of a one-to-one correspondence between a word and its referent, signs may arbitrarily proliferate without any discrete underpinning of meaning.[13] This is the basis of Cipolla's counterfeit operations in language, for he produces signs devoid of significance. When he inveighs against the friars of the "terra di Menzogna" (433) who practice the counterfeiter's art by distributing false indulgences, "nulla altra moneta spendendo che senza conio per quei paesi" (434), we cannot help but read this as self-reflexive. Although Cipolla is following standard homiletic practice, which dictates that a good tirade against the clergy never fails to awaken the congregation, nonetheless his association of verbal falsification ("terra di Menzogna") with counterfeiting is too pointed to ignore. Another allusion to the counterfeiter's art is more subtle, though perhaps Boccaccio's audience would have been quick to apprehend it. In describing Guccio's malice, Cipolla has compared him to Lippo Topo, a contemporary painter famous for his practical jokes, not the least of which was the bequest of large sums of money to all his friends. Since Lippo was known to be a man of modest means, he was asked on his deathbed where this legacy was to be found. The moribund's final words were "Qui sta il punto."[14] Though this light-hearted anecdote scarcely constitutes a case of hard-core counterfeiting, it nevertheless suggests the promise of value where none exists.

Cipolla's primary strategy for the counterfeit production of value is to convert the most banal of quotidian realities into objects of surpassing wonder. A bird's feather becomes a relic of the Angel Gabriel, a lump of coal gains the prestige of an incinerated saint. In the travelogue which comprises the bulk of Cipolla's sermon, Boccaccio reveals the quintessence of this verbal magic when the friar transforms a trek through the streets of Florence into an odyssey of global dimensions.[15] Cipolla can be sure that the provincial Certaldans will not recognize the Florentine street names thinly disguised to produce the most fabulous confusions. He begins his stroll in Via Vinegia and proceeds along Borgo dei Greci, both in the populous zone of Santa Croce. To the Certaldans, however, this would translate into a great oriental leap from Venice to Greece. The next phase of his journey

---

[13] Leo Spitzer's observations on linguistic perspectivism in *Don Quixote* are especially apt to this study. He sees polynomasia as Cervantes' proof of the relativism and instability of human cognition, and of the language which serves as its vehicle. See *Linguistics and Literary History* (Princeton, 1948), pp. 41-85.

[14] See Russo, p. 434.

[15] Here, Cipolla's strategy literalizes the rhetorical category of *digressio*. See Faral, *Les arts poétiques*, pp. 274-275.

would be even more difficult to maneuver, "per lo reame del Garbo, cavalcando e per Baldacca, pervenni in Parione" (433). Though this could be easily executed in Florence, where Cipolla would gallop from Via Condotta, along Via Calimaruzza, to Via Parione, the Certaldans would imagine an itinerary from Africa to Baghdad, to Paris—a ride suitable for the likes of a Pegasus. Thus, a perfectly reasonable jaunt through central Florence becomes a physically impossible tour of the most exotic parts of the world. A similar transformation of the quotidian into the fabulous characterizes Cipolla's anthropological observations. The inhabitants of the Abruzzi exhibit almost extraterrestrial oddity in their social customs, according to this travelogue à la Marco Polo in which wooden shoes, sausages, wine skins, and doughnuts all take on the air of extreme anthropological curiosities.[16]

If a trek through Florence, or the customs of a neighboring province can be transfigured into the marvelous, why not a piece of coal? In its logic, the sanctification of this carbonic lump conforms to the entire course of Cipolla's oration. But we have heard an example of this metamorphizing language already from the mouth of Guccio Imbratta, whose wooings of Nuta read as a deglamorized version of Cipolla's own rhetoric.[17] Guccio faces a challenge as difficult as Cipolla's, for he must transform himself from a specimen of subhuman squalor into a gentleman of means who can advance the fortunes of the unappreciated scullery maid. Boccaccio brutally juxtaposes the reality of Guccio's person with the self-image he "heroically" creates.

> E senza riguardare a un suo cappuccio sopra il quale era tanto untume, che avrebbe condito il calderon d'Altopascio, e a un suo farsetto rotto e ripezzato e intorno al collo e sotto le ditella smaltato di sucidume, con più macchie e di più colori che mai drappi fossero tartereschi o indiani, e alle sue scarpette tutte rotte e alle calze sdrucite, le disse quasi stato fosse il Siri di Ciastiglione, che rivestir la voleva e rimetterla in arnese e trarla di quella cattività di star con altrui e senza gran possession d'avere ridurla in isperanza di miglior fortuna. (431-432)

The first half of this passage mirrors and reverses the second half, suggesting the ironic break between Guccio's self-image and his sordid reality, between his fantasy of power and his true condition of impotence. Boccaccio piles up the nauseating details of Guccio's filth in a series of paratactically ordered phrases connected by polysynde-

---

[16] I, like the Certaldans, needed some help in identifying the true referents of this Cipollan code language. I am indebted to Luigi Russo's annotations, pp. 186-187, for the required identifications.

[17] Several critics have noted how Guccio's rhetoric, and his entire subplot, anticipate Cipolla's own. See Getto, *Vita di forme*, p. 161; Mazzotta, "The Marginality of Literature," p. 74; Borsellino, "*Decameron* come teatro," p. 30; and Baratto, *Realtà e stile*, p. 379.

ton, only to match them with a similarly structured series of promises which Guccio offers Nuta. The first half of the passage gives the lie to the second, even before Guccio has the chance to fail in action. Boccaccio further damns the servant by parodying his own rhetoric of self-glorification. Like his master, Guccio exploits the language of the fantastic for personal gain, flaunting a treasure of "fiorini più di millantanove" and a store of knowledge rivaling "domine pure unquanche" (431). What Boccaccio does is to turn this language of the fantastic back on its exploiter, using exotic allusions to prove the poverty of Guccio's pretensions. His mention of the "calderon d'Altopascio" does not add a fairytale mystique to Guccio's portrait, but reinforces its abject misery, for Altopascio is the almshouse of Lucchesia whose caldron would not be distinguished by its succulent contents.[18] Another exotic allusion which works against Guccio is the comparison of his filth with the variegated fabrics of the Orient. Guccio's complexion is stained with "più colori che mai drappi fossero tartereschi o indiani." This allusion even has the authority of a Dantesque source, for Geryon's coat rivals the most lush eastern imports, "con più color, sommesse e sopraposte/non fer mai drappi Tartari né Turchi" (*Inf.* XVII, 16-17).[19] The Infernal echoes of the comparison accord well with Guccio's own love of smoky subterranean spaces as exemplified by his summer sentinel in Nuta's fetid kitchen ("ancora che d'agosto fosse, postosi presso al fuoco a sedere" 431).

Guccio persists in composing an idealized self-portrait for Nuta, even though she has all the evidence to the contrary before her very eyes. Dressed in his greasy cassock with its threadbare doublet, wearing broken shoes and unraveled socks, his neck and fingernails encrusted with dirt, Guccio nonetheless claims "che egli era gentile uomo per procuratore e che egli aveva de' fiorini più di millantanove, senza quegli che egli aveva a dare altrui, che erano anzi più che meno, e che egli sapeva tante cose fare e dire, che domine pure unquanche" (431). This fourfold repetition of *egli* suggests the infantile narcissism of these muddled statements whose contradictions cancel out any self-serving meaning that would survive the pure nonsense of the whole.

What is Nuta's response to all this? We are never told directly, but can infer from the fact that she has not kicked Guccio out that this suitor's rhetoric has worked. Thus, the kitchen seduction becomes a miniature of Cipolla's con job in church, and Nuta's willingness to entertain Guccio's bluster anticipates the parishioner's acceptance of the friar's verbal constructs. The simplicity of these Certaldans occa-

---

[18] See Russo, p. 182.
[19] Ibid., for the identification of this allusion.

sions some of Boccaccio's least subtle prose, as he feels no need to ironize their flaws. They are "sciocchi" (429), "semplici" (432), and offer "buona pastura" (429) for Cipolla's fiscal harvest. Boccaccio suggests that the Certaldans possess subhuman intelligence, identifying them with the very beasts which Sant'Antonio promises to protect ("il beato santo Antonio vi sia guardia de' buoi e degli asini e de' porci e delle pecore vostre" 430) and similar to Ciappelletto's worshippers in I, 1, they mob the friar like a stampeding herd ("con grandissima calca" 435).

There is a second public in this story, no less admiring of the friar than the first, but far more enlightened. This is the public of Cipolla's own personal *brigata*, and it includes Giovanni del Bragoniera and Biagio Pizzini, the two pranksters who put the friar's extemporizing powers to the test.[20] Throughout the tale, we view the action from the perspective of these troublemakers who know the secret of Cipolla's hypocrisy. That shared perspective makes us members of Cipolla's *brigata*. Boccaccio reinforces our membership by a certain kind of name dropping: when he alludes to the figures of Lippo Topo and Maso del Saggio without any prior exposition, he assumes that we know these famous practical jokesters already, and that we are part of the world which values witty reprisal as the supreme measure of civic virtue. Boccaccio seems to be erecting here a kind of pranksters' Hall of Fame and assuring our acquaintance with its principals.

Thus, our perspective is identified with that of the members of Cipolla's *brigata* and we watch with them as the friar extricates himself from an impossible bind with the most extraordinary improvisations. At the end of the tale, this second public separates itself off from the gullible crowd to congratualte the super-jokester, who has not only defrauded the masses, but outwitted his outwitters. "E poi che partito si fu il vulgo, a lui andatisene, con la maggior festa del mondo ciò che fatto avevan gli discoprirono e appresso gli renderono la sua penna" (436).

Together with this second public, we are privy to the relativity of language which makes possible Cipolla's achievement. We realize that the friar's locutions point to no truth beyond themselves, that he distorts, through language, the data of the objective world to serve his own venal ends. His long and convoluted pilgrimage from "Vinegia" to the Holy Land, in which Florentine street names are thinly disguised to suggest the remote and the unfamiliar, is more than a psychological diversion for his public. The journey betrays the dis-

---

[20] The privileged perspective of these two pranksters is noted by Mazzotta in "The Marginality of Literature," p. 75.

tance Cipolla has strayed from true meaning. This physical wandering has a moral dimension as well—it is an *errare* from straightforward signification, as the friar twists verbal signs from authentic meaning to one which satisfies erroneous desires. Following his midsermon discovery of the coals, Cipolla realizes that he must take his listeners on a journey into error, leading them astray so that they will accept the forgery he will hand them in the putative coals of San Lorenzo.[21]

To appreciate the full extent of Cipolla's errancy, we must bear in mind that he is no ordinary con man, but a member of the clergy whose position gives his deviance an added dimension. For Cipolla has not only strayed from true signification, he has made a mockery of God's own mode of signifying through the Incarnation. At the end of Cipolla's journey to the Holy Land awaits an inventory of relics which are all distortions of the incarnational ideal—a finger of the Holy Ghost, a Seraphic forelock, a Cherubic fingernail, a rib of the Logos, some clothing of the personified Faith, rays from the Eastern Star, sweat from the Archangel Michael—all "embodiments" of pure spirit. By corporealizing the incorporeal, the friar usurps a divine prerogative and calls down upon himself the inescapable charge of idolatry. Cipolla's choice of the Angel Gabriel as his putative feather-bearer reinforces this idolatrous mimesis of divine operations. As Gabriel's word announced the incarnation of the Logos, Cipolla's allusion to the archangel on the morning of his sermon adumbrates his own donation of bodies to creatures of pure spirit in his list of invented relics.

Names in Boccaccio are seldom mere tags of identification. Often they perform a descriptive or explanatory function by pointing to an aspect of the name-bearer which fails to emerge in dialogue, action, or direct expository passages. We have seen how Ser Ciappelletto's name recapitulates the distortions and misunderstandings which led the local parish to canonize a sinner. Frate Cipolla's name serves a similar descriptive purpose—one which will require a look at medieval botanical tradition in order to discern its subtle logic.

Theophrastus, whose *Enquiry into Plants* exerted considerable influence on subsequent botanical studies, gives some attention to the multiple skins of the onion.[22] This feature becomes a commonplace in

---

[21] In her article "Saint Augustine's Region of Unlikeness: The Crossing of Exile and Language," *The Georgia Review*, 29 (Winter 1975), Margaret Ferguson treats erring as a linguistic phenomenon. Hence, figurative language is seen as a deviation from straightforward signification (p. 844), though, according to Augustine, even literal language is guilty of such errancy (p. 856).

[22] Theophrastus lists the onion among those plants which have manifold layers of skin. "Again in some the bark has more than one layer as in lime, silver-fir, vine, Spanish

Renaissance herbals,[23] and gives rise to a figurative meaning of special importance to our study. In the history of connotations assigned to *la cipolla* we read: "fig. a indicare grossolanità d'anima, doppiezza, falsità." Hence the idiom "falso come una cipolla" means "persona falsa, ipocrita (immagine ricavata dalla composizione a vari strati della cipolla")." [24] The fact that the Florentine barber and poet Domenico di Giovanni, known as Il Burchiello, used the onion as a metaphor for duplicity ("egli è doppio più ch'una cipolla") in the early fifteenth century suggests that this figurative meaning has a long Tuscan history. Thus Cipolla's name becomes an elaborate literary joke, serving as an organic metaphor for the very linguistic relativity which governs his discourse. Like the onion with its manifold skins and seedless center, Cipolla's rhetoric contains layer upon layer of identical signs which harbor no underlying truth.

Boccaccio's choice of the onion as his controlling image suggests a theory of fiction radically different from that set forth in the *De genealogia*. Had he chosen a conventional fruit, with a rind protecting a pulp and a seed, he would have approximated imagistically the argument for an allegorical reading of fiction which he advances in the philological text. Throughout the *De genealogia*, Boccaccio defends the dignity of fictional constructs by insisting upon the existence of a meaning hidden beneath the poetic surface. As discussed earlier, a sharp differentiation between the figurative and literal orders enables Boccaccio to disclaim the charges of frivolity and seduction which had been leveled against the poets. "You added a further request, that I explain the meaning which wise men had hidden under this cover of absurd tales," [25] Boccaccio states in his preface to the *De genealogia*. This duality recurs in a further definition: "whatever is composed as under a veil, and thus exquisitely wrought is poetry and poetry alone." [26] And again, "fiction is a form of discourse which, under guise of invention, illustrates or proves an idea; and as its superficial aspect

broom, onions" (35). When another plant exhibits similar stratification, Theophrastus compares it to the onion. "Moreover, the wood of the silver-fir has many layers, like an onion." See *Enquiry into Plants*, trans. Sir Arthur Holt (London and New York, 1916), I, 423.

[23] In *De historia stirpium commentarii insignes* (London, 1555), Leonard Fuchs gives a somewhat detailed anatomy of the bulb. "Capitatam (habet) pluribus compactam tunicis, quae summatim praetenuibis, rufisq, vestitur membranis" (480). John Gerard goes into similar detail in his description of the onion in *The Herball or General History of Plants* (London, 1597). "Insteede of the roote there is a bulbe or round head compact of many coates . . . it is covered with very fine skins for the most part of a whitish colour" (134).

[23] *Grande dizionario della lingua italiana*, III, 172.

[25] Osgood, *Boccaccio on Poetry*, p. 6.

[26] Ibid., p. 42.

is removed, the meaning of the author is clear."[27] Other such incentives to a twofold reading of fiction are scattered throughout the *De genealogia*, making this Boccaccio's primary defense against the poet-haters who would reduce their reading to a one-dimensional exercise in literal-mindedness.

But Cipolla's onion-like rhetoric yields no such twofold reading. His fictions do not hide a superior truth, they hide only more fictions, producing an infinite regress of signs without content. At the center of this onion lies an empty reliquary, "la cassetta vota" (432), which serves as the prototype of all elements in Cipolla's rhetorical system. When the friar explains to his congregation that a confusion in reliquaries caused him to mistake one for the other, he is betraying the essential nonspecificity of his language whose words, like the containers "son sì simiglianti l'una all'altra, che spesse volte mi vien presa l'una per l'altra, e al presente m'è avvenuto: per ciò che, credendomi io qui avere arrecata la cassetta dove era la penna, io ho arrecata quella dove sono i carboni" (435). The redundancy of this explanation ("l'una all'altra . . . l'una per l'altra . . . arrecata la cassetta dove . . . arrecata quella dove") reinforces our sense of the absolute interchangeability of all elements in this rhetoric. The identical reliquaries are like Cipolla's words—empty signifiers, indifferent to content and hence resistant to meaning.[28]

Perhaps Giovanni del Bragoniera and Biagio Pizzini would have succeeded in exposing Cipolla's ruse had they left the container empty instead of refilling it with coals. But this carbonic substitute enables Cipolla to generate another fiction and thus to save face before the expectant crowd. Even if we were to rewrite the story leaving the container empty, who knows if Frate Cipolla would not have found in it some airy relic: a sigh of Maria, or a sneeze of the Holy Ghost?

But what about Boccaccio? Is he too engulfed by Cipolla's linguistic vacuum? When the writer says that his home town Certaldo is famous for its onions ("con ciò sia cosa che quel terreno produca cipolle famose per tutta Toscana" 429), is he including himself in this harvest of Cipollan hypocrites?

Obviously Boccaccio's language does aspire to meaning, if only to show how other people's language does not.[29] This exposé of the

[27] Ibid., p. 48.

[28] In *"Decameron* come teatro," pp. 28-29, Borsellino notes the connection between the interchangeable relics and the interchangeable words of Cipolla's lexicon.

[29] By exposing the instability and untrustworthiness of language, and then using it as an instrument of truth, Boccaccio is working in a classical tradition, as Ferguson describes it in "Saint Augustine's Region of Unlikeness," pp. 847-848.

storyteller *in malo* reveals by contrast Boccaccio's radically opposed
linguistic strategy. By making his protagonist's name signify what he
is, Boccaccio exemplifies the Realists' dictum *nomina sunt consequentia
rerum*. But this is not a Realism that points to any system of objective
truth beyond the narration. Instead, it emerges from the context of
the tale itself as Cipolla's own antics conspire to prove the propriety of
his name. Implicit in this very designation is the dichotomy between
the protagonist's language and Boccaccio's own: the former dedicated
to hide the void at its center; the latter determined to expose it. In the
two publics generated by Cipolla's example, Boccaccio reveals the
dramatic results of these divergent rhetorical practices. There are the
Certaldans who leave the friar's performance *crociati, rubati, e ingan-
nati*; and ourselves, who emerge from the story better and wiser readers, alert to the abuses of language, and wary of the more subtle and
dangerous Cipollas in our own midst.

V

MISCHIEF AND MISBELIEF

THE FIRST TALE OF CALANDRINO (VIII, 3)

Boccaccio has made the perils of gullibility an underlying theme of the entire text, from the literal-minded parishioners who took Ser Ciappelletto and Fra Cipolla at their word, to the brainless and narcissistic Madonna Lisetta (IV, 2) who believed that the Angel Gabriel had taken on hands, feet, and other organs, in order to enjoy her embraces. There is, of course, a lesson for the reader in these examples of credulity exploited, for Boccaccio never ceases to remind us that his text is an artifact like those of the fiction makers within its pages, and that we must heed the consequences of literal-mindedness on the variously duped victims of the stories. Boccaccio underscores this warning to the reader by gathering a closely knit listening public around the figure who is to be the very apotheosis of gullibility in Days VIII and IX—the lovable but dull-witted Calandrino. No other character inspires such enthusiasm and delight in the *brigata* as this naïf who becomes the protagonist of four separate tales, told by four separate tellers, scattered over the course of two days.[1]

Although Boccaccio does not juxtapose these tales one after another, he clearly intends that they be read as a coherent unit, forming a serialized portrait of gullibility in all its possible permutations. Since we already know the characters, settings, and the basic sequence

---

[1] Russo, in *Il Decameron*, p. 443; Almansi, in *The Writer as Liar*, p. 75; and Battaglia, in *La coscienza letteraria del medioevo* (Naples, 1965), p. 701; all comment on the episodic appearances of Calandrino, and hence the existence of a Calandrino cycle. Actually, the Calandrino sequence spreads beyond the four tales in which he is specifically featured, since Bruno and Buffalmacco, Calandrino's constant tormentors, also appear in another tale, VIII, 9, and Maso del Saggio, who makes a brief but significant appearance in the opening Calandrino tale, is mentioned by Fra Cipolla in VI, 10 and becomes the protagonist of his own tale in VIII, 5.

of events after reading the first Calandrino tale, we can then concentrate our energies on the variations and nuances which Boccaccio is able to work into this repeated theme. Thus, our response to the Calandrino sequence will be different from our response to the rest of the text whose very heterogeneity has dramatized the difference, contradiction, and irreducibility of human experience. Here, instead, we focus on the rigidity and coherence of a protagonist who refuses to recognize the signs of inevitable entrapment.

It is the characters themselves who point out the continuity of the Calandrino cycle as they refer back to previous tales to justify the latest punishment which the protagonist's simplicity has merited. The characters in VIII, 6 claim that the events of VIII, 3 warrant their current revenge, while those in IX, 5 allude to two earlier tales, VIII, 3 and IX, 3, to explain the justice of Calandrino's final punishment at the hands of his outraged wife. The frame story *brigata* also calls our attention to the continuity of the Calandrino sequence by "apologizing" for its redundancy with arguments so flimsy and insincere that they only serve to heighten our awareness of the very repetition they regret. What we sense, instead, is the pride and delight of the *brigata* in being able to multiply stories of Calandrino, the mere mention of whose name sets off a series of associations in the minds of the storytellers, and a chain reaction of related tales. The readiness with which these stories are produced suggests that they come from a preexisting fund of Calandrino lore—one in which the entire *brigata* shares as part of its cultural heritage. The telling of these tales thus binds the *brigata* together by demonstrating its possession of a common folk culture, replete with heroes, victims, and in-jokes.

The *brigata*, however, shares more than the content of its cultural lore—it also shares a certain perspective on it. When the storytellers delight in the exploits and mishaps of the lower classes, they do so from the position of a cultural elite whose amusement takes into account the considerable class distance between the object of laughter and those who are doing the laughing.[2] The Calandrino tales thus have a function similar to ethnic jokes in our culture, defining the tellers as a community in two ways: first as socially separate from the butt of the joke, and second as sharers in a common fund of cultural lore.

The Florentine setting of the Calandrino tales underscores their immediacy for the storytelling *brigata*. In fact, the opening words of the first Calandrino story announce that these will be particularly

---

[2] The classist condescension which the *brigata* shows toward this popular material dramatizes, according to Sapegno, Boccaccio's own artistic detachment from his work. See *Il Trecento*, p. 348.

Sacchetti.
Bocc's
Calandrino
cycle as
model.

"Florentine" tales, set as they are "nella nostra città" (514).[3] The use of the first person plural of the possessive pronoun immediately implicates the listeners in the world of this tale, creating them as a community in their collective knowledge of this particular side of Florence, the Florence "di varie maniere e di nuove genti" (514). In making this saga of practical joking an intimately "Florentine" tale, Boccaccio is developing a motif he inherited from the author of the *Novellino*. The tale in that earlier collection, which may be seen as the pilot for this entire subgenre of tales about tricksters and rogues, is Florentine to the utmost. Its protagonist, the forerunner of the Brunos and Buffalmaccos of *Decameron* fame, is introduced thus: "Bito fue fiorentino"[4] as if such information were enough to suggest the passion for practical jokes which will typify this culture. The tale of Bito's treachery to the miserly Ser Frulli is so intimately associated with the map of Florence that it seems expressly written for her citizens, since only they could appreciate the subtleties of her fine intraurban distinctions. The author of the *Novellino* dramatizes the special appeal of this tale to a Florentine public by building one into the narration itself, making the local witnesses to Bito's prank an important part of the comic resolution. By siding with Bito against Ser Frulli, and sanctioning the hero's somewhat cruel devices, this public ratifies the justice of an otherwise gratuitous prank.

Boccaccio has followed a similar, though more complex strategy in the tale of Fra Cipolla, for this introduction into the sophisticated subculture of practical jokers, with its *brigate*, its folk heroes, and its own system of distributive justice, is ideally suited to a Florentine public. Only a Florentine, or one well acquainted with the plan of the city, would understand the allusions to local street names which constitute the wit of Cipolla's itinerary to the Holy Land. A Florentine public would also enjoy Boccaccio's references to the provincial ignorance of the Certaldans, and to their double defeat at the hands of one obviously well versed in the cosmopolitan art of the "con."

Four decades later, Franco Sacchetti will confirm the success of this Florentine storytelling mode by filling his *Trecentonovelle* with tales of pranks engineered by, for, and amidst Florentines. This particular strain of Boccaccio's heterogeneous art becomes the whole of Sacchetti's, dedicated as it is to that cult of the idiosyncratic, the bizarre, the *nuovo* which Boccaccio embodied in Calandrino. That Florence which Sacchetti makes the very subject of his narration is modeled on Calandrino's city, "la qual sempre di varie maniere e di nuove genti è

---

[3] For a fuller discussion of the "Florentinity" of these tales, see Baratto, *Realtà e stile*, p. 67.
[4] *Novellino*, p. 204.

stata abondevole" (514). When Sacchetti echoes this description in the "città di Firenze, che sempre di nuovi uomeni è stata doviziosa,"[5] he signals his intention to perfect not only Calandrino's Florence, but also that storytelling genre which has immortalized it.

In the opening line of the first Calandrino tale, Boccaccio twice uses an adjective which will enjoy good fortune with Sacchetti. That is the adjective *nuovo* with which Boccaccio describes both the general population of Florence and Calandrino himself, thereby suggesting a synecdochic relationship between the protagonist and his city. "Nella nostra città, la qual sempre di varie maniere e di nuove genti è stata abondevole, fu, ancora non è gran tempo, un dipintore chiamato Calandrino, uom semplice e di nuovi costumi" (514). Boccaccio here introduces the general theme of novelty which the rest of the tale will illustrate in the astonishing behaviors of Calandrino. But Boccaccio's use of the term is itself an example of the very novelty it comes to signify, for the writer utilizes it in an unorthodox way, emptying it of any traditional normative content, and then making it the basis for the pranksters' new ethos of credulity and cunning.

For Dante, the notion of novelty carried a strong moral charge. His conservatism led him to condemn all social change on *a priori* grounds, making political history a steady movement away from the perfection of an irrevocable past. Thus, when three denizens of the seventh circle ask Dante for news about contemporary Florence, the pilgrim inveighs:

> La gente nova e i subiti guadagni
> orgoglio e dismisura han generata,
> Fiorenza, in te, sì che tu già ten piagni.
> (*Inf.* XVI, 73-75)

Fresh from his encounter with Brunetto Latini in *Inferno* XV, Dante echoes his master's xenophobia when he regrets the contamination of the ancient Roman stock by newcomers from Fiesole. Dante uses the term *nova* in a double sense, describing not only the people who are newly arrived, but also the aberration from a historical norm which this influx of a non-Roman population would imply.

Boccaccio, instead, depoliticizes the concept of "nuove genti," making it the object of polite entertainment, and not of partisan invective. This "rifiuto di parlare di politica," as Franco Fido calls it, may reflect the storyteller's general dislike of overt didacticism, or his reluctance to remind the Florentine burghers that they themselves were "nuove genti" not so very long ago.[6] Boccaccio thus rejects the moral judg-

---

[5]   Franco Sacchetti, *Trecentonovelle*, ed. Vincenzo Pernicone (Florence, 1946), p. 300.

[6]   Fido, "Dante, personaggio mancato del *Decameron*," in *Le metamorfosi del centauro: Studi*

ments implicit in Dante's theme of novelty, and replaces them with a new, unorthodox ethical code which rewards wit and punishes gullibility, regardless of the moral ends so served. Distributive justice is meted out with exactitude, but the categories of good and bad which predominate in the surrounding social order are replaced by those of cunning and naiveté in this community of tricksters, con artists, and their dupes.[7] Variations of the term *nuovo* thus appear three times in the opening passage of the first Calandrino tale, suggesting the peculiar dynamic of this pranksters' paradise. Novelty is attributed to the victim, to the prank, and to the entire subculture which nourishes such conduct. Accordingly, Calandrino is labeled a man "di nuovi costumi" (514) who inspires the contrivance of "alcuna nuova cosa" (514) by the notorious prankster Maso del Saggio. The term thus embraces the cunning of Maso and the simplicity of Calandrino— seemingly antithetical notions which Boccaccio shows to be interdependent by ascribing the same adjective to both. The word assumes its synthetic value when applied to that Florence which supplies an abundance of tricksters and their dupes. Only at the end of the tale does the theme of novelty recur, this time in the term *novella*, which is derived, of course, from the root word *nuovo*. When Bruno and Buffalmacco behold the violent consequences of their prank on Tessa, the victimized wife of Calandrino, they ask the battered woman "che novelle son queste?" (519). Here the term best approximates the English word *news*, i.e., those events which are both real, yet extraordinary—in short, "something worth telling."[8] The *novelle* which meet Bruno's and Buffalmacco's eyes upon entering the rooms of their outraged friend and his pulverized wife seem to sum up all the fantastic, bizarre behaviors which have led up to this squalid

---

e letture da Boccaccio a Pirandello (Rome, 1977), p. 86. Muscetta, however, in *Lettura militante* (Florence, 1953), attributes the novel behaviors of the Calandrinos of Florence to their recent arrival in the city and their quests for instant cosmopolitanism. Tateo also sees in Boccaccio's use of the term *nuovo* a political meaning: the confrontation of the old feudal world with the new bourgeoisie. See "Il 'realismo' nella novella boccaccesca," p. 181.

[7] In "Forms of Accommodation in the *Decameron*," p. 305, Greene reconciles these tales of jests for their own sake with his overall reading of the *Decameron* as an affirmation of the social order by seeing in Calandrino's dull-wittedness a "social irritant" which Bruno and Buffalmacco set out to purge. For an analysis of Boccaccio's system of distributive justice, see Scaglione, *Nature and Love*, pp. 92-93.

[8] See Maurice Valency's introduction to *The Palace of Pleasure: An Anthology of the Novella*, ed. M. Valency and H. Levtow (New York, 1960), p. 1. For a reading of the *Decameron novella* as a mixture of the quotidian and the extraordinary, I am indebted to the ideas presented by Walter Davis in his paper "Boccaccio: The Implications of Binary Form" presented at the Thirteenth Annual Conference of Medieval Studies sponsored by the Medieval Institute at Kalamazoo, Michigan, on May 4, 1978.

scene—a conclusion which not even the two pranksters had anticipated. And yet the tale has been firmly grounded in the real—a recognizable Florence in a recognizable time in her history, populated by
characters whose historicity is a matter of public record.[9] The occurrence of the term *novelle* at the end of this tale may have a metaliterary
resonance, suggesting the species of story Boccaccio had in mind
when he offered the term as one of the synonyms for storytelling in
his proem ("intendo di raccontare cento novelle, o favole o parabole o
istorie che dire le vogliamo" 4). The *novella* may be a precise label for
stories about the "nuove genti" of Calandrino's world, recording the
interdependence of pranksters and victims in the cult of the practical
joke. If this is so, then the first Calandrino tale of the *Decameron* can be
read as the prototype of the *novella* understood in this strict sense,
offering a key to the dynamic of subsequent *novelle*, both of the
Calandrino cycle, and of Days VIII and IX as a whole.

The first tale of Calandrino divides neatly into two parts, as Luigi
Russo observes,[10] corresponding to the two separate pranks which
constitute the plot. The first is a verbal one, and it is administered by
Maso del Saggio who convinces Calandrino of the existence of that
glutton's paradise: the land of Bengodi, with its mountains of grated
cheese, its rivers of Vernaccia, and its perpetual avalanches of pasta.
As Russo points out, the first part of the Calandrino tale is in many
ways an extension of Fra Cipolla's, for Maso uses the same verbal
techniques that the friar did to hoodwink his parish.[11] Thus, when
Calandrino asks Maso if he has ever been to Bengodi, the trickster
replies "sì vi sono stato così una volta come mille" (515), using Fra
Cipolla's technique of self-canceling rhetoric which denies an assertion as soon as it is made. The same ploy is used when Calandrino asks
if Bengodi is far beyond the Abruzzi, which has for him the remote-
ness and exoticism of the Himalayas, and Maso answers "sì bene . . .
sì è cavelle" (515). When asked about the distance to Bengodi, Maso
echoes Cipolla's use of authoritative-sounding nonsense by saying
"haccene più di millanta, che tutta notte canta" (515).[12] And as Cipolla
made the most unremarkable facts into items of surpassing wonder,
so Maso tells Calandrino of the magical stones in nearby Settignano
and Montisci which have the power to grind wheat into flour, and so

---

[9] For the historical counterparts of Calandrino, Tessa, Bruno, and Buffalmacco, see
Russo, *Il Decameron*, pp. 191-192.

[10] Russo divides the tale into an introductory part, dominated by Maso del Saggio, and
the actual body of the tale, dominated by Calandrino himself. See pp. 451-452.

[11] Ibid., p. 451. On this same page, Russo analyzes the Cipollan rhetoric of Maso's
dialogue with Calandrino.

[12] Actually, *millanta* is used by Cipolla's servant, Guccio, but it reflects the friar's own
use of mystifying rhetoric to impress his credulous hearers.

he tells the simpleton that the more ravioli one gathers in Bengodi, the more one has ("chi più ne pigliava più se n'aveva" 515) and that he who bears the heliotrope is not seen where he is not ("non è da alcuna altra persona veduto dove non è" 516). Maso even coins a proverb to lend authority to his observations about grindstones: "per ciò si dice egli in que' paesi di là che da Dio vengon le grazie e da Montisci le macine" (515-516).[13]

This first part of the tale, wherein Maso sows the seed for the actual prank that Bruno and Buffalmacco will play on Calandrino in part two, is perhaps longer than the exigencies of the plot would require. The figure of Maso is an extraneous one, for Boccaccio could have made Bruno and Buffalmacco the source of the heliotrope idea, as well as the executors of the prank itself. But by separating the preparatory part of the hoax from its execution, and by giving a separate character the task of planting the seed in Calandrino's mind, Boccaccio dramatizes the onset of Calandrino's misbelief and calls attention to its peculiar dynamic. The protagonist's predisposition to delusion and the birth of this particular delusional system thus become part of the primary subject matter of this opening Calandrino tale, preparing us for the artistry of the deception to come.

Part two of the tale commences with Calandrino's rush to include Bruno and Buffalmacco ("li quali spezialissimamente amava" 516) in his quest for the heliotrope. He is smitten by the idea of the magical powers that this stone will confer on its bearer and proposes that he and his two comrades rob the local money-changers while cloaked in the garb of invisibility. Bruno and Buffalmacco are delighted to go along with this intrigue and the three arrange to meet at the riverbed of the Mugnone on Sunday morning, when Calandrino will collect every stone which shows the slightest resemblance to Maso's description of the heliotrope. Now it is time for Bruno and Buffalmacco to convince Calandrino that he is invisible, and they do so by pretending to have lost him when he is obviously in their midst. Calandrino decides not to share this newly found power with his friends, and pays a high price for his selfishness by having to remain silent while Bruno and Buffalmacco pelt him with stones. The customs officers at the city gate have been forewarned of the jest, and they reinforce the illusion of Calandrino's invisibility by feigning not to see him. Since it is lunch time, the passersby are few, and they do not acknowledge Calandrino's presence, so he is convinced more than ever of his transparency. It is Tessa's misfortune to be the first to see him, since Calan-

---

[13] In *"Decameron come teatro,"* pp. 27-28, Borsellino interprets Maso's nonsense replies to Calandrino as theatrical devices to invoke public complicity.

drino is certain that she has broken the heliotrope's spell, but Bruno and Buffalmacco arrive just in time to prevent irreparable damage, and they manage to sober Calandrino by blaming him for the improvidence of appearing before a woman, knowing full well that "le femine fanno perder la vertù a ogni cosa" (520).

Part of the joke on Calandrino is that what he considers to be the latest revelation of lapidary science really has a long and ambiguous history, as Pliny reveals in his entry on heliotropes in the *Historiae naturalis*.[14] "In the use of this stone, also, we have a most glaring illustration of the impudent effrontery of the adepts in magic, for they say that, if it is combined with the plant heliotropium, and certain incantations are then repeated over it, it will render a person invisible who carries it about with him."[15] Despite Pliny, popular tradition continued to give the heliotrope its magical powers, as the author of the *Novellino* attests. His very first tale elevates this datum of lapidary lore from the level of folk wisdom to that of kingly *saviezza*. According to this story, Prester John sends the Emperor Frederick three gems, including a heliotrope, to test his reputation for learning, but the Emperor disappoints him by neglecting to inquire about their hidden virtues. Fearing that the stones will lose their powers from disuse, Prester John commissions his personal jeweler to recover them from Frederick. The jeweler insinuates himself into the Emperor's court, asks to see and handle the gems, becomes invisible, and is able to spirit the treasure back to Prester John.

Although Frederick is presented as a paragon of chivalric virtue ("specchio del mondo in parlare e in costumi"),[16] his failure to inquire into the hidden powers of the gift jewels injures his performance in Prester John's test of *saviezza*. It is the jeweler who emerges truly *savio*, for his wisdom extends beyond external forms to the underlying, and most efficacious truths. His act of disappearance by means of the heliotrope is the ultimate manipulation of appearances, and the strongest argument against trusting exclusively in them.

Now Boccaccio reverses the outcome of the *Novellino* tale by making disbelief in the heliotrope the test of true *saviezza*. Frederick fails his intelligence test by doubting the power of the stone, while Calandrino fails by believing it. Yet Calandrino and the Emperor partake of the same error in that they both trust implicitly in appearances: the Emperor neglecting to go beyond the physical surface of the stone to consider its hidden virtues; Calandrino neglecting to go beyond the

---

[14] Attilio Hortis documents Boccaccio's knowledge of this work. See *Studj sulle opere latine del Boccaccio* (Trieste, 1879), pp. 433-434.

[15] *The Natural History of Pliny*, trans. John Bostock, H.R. Riley (London, 1857), VI, 450.

[16] *Novellino*, p. 64.

surface of Maso's lie to discover its patent nontruth. While rejecting
the letter of the *Novellino* story, then, Boccaccio retains its underlying
meaning (the mistrust of the obvious). He thus enacts that very lesson
in his relationship to his literary model, going beyond the literal level
of this source to less obvious, and more precious truths.

Calandrino's initial appearance in the tale is a crucial one, for it
reveals his vulnerability to deception and suggests to Maso the precise
tactics he must follow in realizing the full potential of this perfect
dupe: "E per avventura trovandolo un dì nella chiesa di San Giovanni
e vedendolo stare attento a riguardare le dipinture e gl'intagli del
tabernaculo il quale è sopra l'altare della detta chiesa, non molto
tempo davanti postovi, pensò essergli dato luogo e tempo alla sua
intenzione" (514). It is Calandrino's rapt attention to these painted
and sculpted images which convinces Maso that his target will be an
easy one. But to test the limits of Calandrino's gullibility before setting
the final trap, Maso weaves the fiction of Bengodi. Calandrino's credulity proves infinite, as his initial absorption in the artifacts of San
Giovanni had led Maso to suspect. "Calandrino semplice, veggendo
Maso dir queste parole con un viso fermo e senza ridere, quella fede vi
dava che dar si può a qualunque verità è più manifesta, e così l'aveva
per vere" (515). Thus, Calandrino is seduced by the appearance of
truth ("qualunque verità è *più manifesta*"), never probing beneath the
surface to explore the disparate meanings which appearances often
belie. His artistic profession reinforces this emphasis on surfaces, as
he himself laments when he promises Bruno and Buffalmacco wealth
enough to save them from the crustacean fate of the fresco painters.
"E così potremo arricchire subitamente, senza avere tutto dì a
schicchera re le mura a modo che fa la lumaca" (516). It is significant
that Calandrino's profession is the manufacture of visual images, and
that his absorption in the artifacts of San Giovanni is a visual one. For
the wit of this tale resides in the various uses of the verb *vedere*, and in
Calandrino's failure to distinguish between them. Although Boccaccio
uses *vedere* to signify seeing, seeming, and understanding, in separate
and distinct contexts, Calandrino insists on combining all three meanings so that sense impressions immediately become the stuff of understanding without any intervening acts of judgment or discrimination.
Calandrino thus collapses the gradations of medieval psychology into
one, homogeneous level, equating the sensitive and intellective faculties which should be ordered in a strict hierarchy of importance.

Early in the tale, Boccaccio introduces the word play which will
culminate in Calandrino's illusion of invisibility.[17] Maso has spotted

---

[17] For a more extensive survey of the antithesis *vedere-non vedere* in this tale, see Marga
Cottino-Jones, "Magic and Superstition," pp. 19-20.

his prey in San Giovanni, and convinces the simpleton that he is in the presence of "un solenne e gran lapidario" (515) by conducting learned discussions about the mineral science within earshot of Calandrino. In order to persuade him that this is not a contrived performance, but a genuine show of expertise, Maso and his uniden-tified accomplice must feign ignorance of Calandrino's presence. And they do so, "faccendo vista di non vederlo" (514). This pretense of not seeing Calandrino is prophetic of the heliotrope episode to come, when Bruno and Buffalmacco will convince the simpleton of his transparancy by using precisely the same ploy.

Calandrino believes this visual construct which Maso has contrived to persuade the protagonist that he is unnoticed. But the pretense of not seeing Calandrino is itself an artifact, a lie which replaces the truth with a clever simulacrum. Just as Calandrino had been enthralled by the painted images of San Giovanni, he is now captivated by Maso's visual construct which mediates and distorts his perception of events. This is also how Bruno and Buffalmacco will persuade Calandrino of his invisibility in the Mugnone, as will the customs officers at the city gates who are accomplices in deception. To these last, Boccaccio will attribute the phrase which has revealed the visual strategy of Maso's earlier pretense: "faccendo vista di non vedere" (518). Once Calan-drino has been made "visible" again through the unexpected agency of his wife, Bruno and Buffalmacco perpetuate the illusion of his past invisibility by two more visual constructs, each of which is signaled by the formula *fare vista*. Thus, the two pranksters pretend to have ar-rived from the Mugnone just at that moment, "faccendo vista di giu-gnere pure allora" (519), although they had in truth tarried with the customs officers at the city gates, and thus when Calandrino narrates the tale of his disappearance under the auspices of the heliotrope, Bruno and Buffalmacco feign the appropriate surprise, "facevan vista di maravigliarsi forte" (520). But these devices cannot affect Calan-drino's awareness of his present state, for Tessa has given him a reaction which is unmediated by any visual construct. Angry that he has returned home late for lunch, she makes no bones about seeing him, and so the spell of the heliotrope is broken. "Veggendo che veduto era" (519) Calandrino knows that he is visible once more, since there is no mediating illusion or device to tell him otherwise.

It is the two pranksters who give *vedere* its decisive meaning—one that reveals the corrective for Calandrino's gullibility. In the variant *avvedersi* and its noun *avvedimento*, Bruno and Buffalmacco suggest the very virtue in which Calandrino is so woefully lacking: that faculty of awareness which allows us to see through the obvious, to anticipate a time beyond the immediate present, to see with the eyes of the mind, and not simply with those of the body. At the very start of the tale, Boccaccio had introduced the two pranksters as "avveduti" (514), and now at the story's end, that faculty is put to a rigorous test. Bruno and Buffalmacco must save Tessa from a second beating at the hands of her enraged husband, while at the same time sustaining Calandrino's belief in the heliotrope fiction.[18] They do so by faulting Calandrino for his lack of "avvedimento" (520) in allowing himself to appear before Tessa when he knew "che le femine facevano perdere la vertù alle cose" (520). Bruno and Buffalmacco even go so far as to see in Calandrino's disappointment a divine punishment for his refusal to share the discovery of the heliotrope with his friends. Such is the pranksters' genius that it not only salvages their trick from an unexpectedly violent end, but also turns this fiction into a morality tale against the sin of avarice. Bruno and Buffalmacco show ample evidence of the *avvedimento* which Calandrino lacks in this master stroke of improvisation and wit.

But our study would remain incomplete without further consideration of the heliotrope, for Boccaccio's logic in choosing this stone is more than meets the eye. It is not just the reputation for magical powers which recommends the heliotrope to this story, but certain natural properties as well. According to Pliny,

> it (the heliotrope) has been thus named from the circumstance that, if placed in a vessel of water and exposed to the full light of the sun, it changes to a reflected colour like that of blood, this being the case with the stone of Aethopia more particularly. Out of the water, too, it reflects the figure of the sun like a mirror, and it discovers eclipses of that luminary by showing the moon passing over its disk.[19]

The heliotrope thus acts like a reflecting surface whose appearance is determined by an external source of light. Now the joke in Calandrino's quest for the heliotrope becomes clearer. Whereas the protagonist thinks that possession of the stone will confer upon him magical powers, he has really taken on its natural, reflective properties. For Calandrino's self-image is derived exclusively from without—he is what others believe him to be. Thus, when Bruno and Buffalmacco act as if Calandrino were invisible, the simpleton believes he is just that, and when Tessa indicates that she sees him, Calandrino conceives of himself as visible once again. His knowledge of his condition is always mediated by others, so he has no direct, empirical experience

[18] Getto admires the persistence of Bruno and Buffalmacco in maintaining the joke to the end. See *Vita di forme*, p. 186.
[19] *The Natural History of Pliny*, p. 450. For medieval interpretations of the heliotrope's powers, see Lynn Thorndike, *A History of Magic and of Experimental Science*, II (New York, 1923), 361, 363, 429, 470, 960.

of his own being. The heliotrope, then, becomes an objective correlative for this man whose self is a reflection of what others seem to see in him.

Calandrino's gullibility resides in precisely this commitment of his identity to others, leaving him with no absolute and autonomous sense of self. Like the heliotrope whose appearance will depend upon the quality of sunlight to which it is exposed, so Calandrino's identity will be determined by external circumstances entirely beyond his control, primarily the wit and whim of his mischievous friends. In another tale, we shall see the extremes to which Bruno's and Buffalmacco's power over Calandrino will go, when the naïf is convinced by his colleagues' feigned solicitude that he is not only pale and wan, but pregnant (IX, 3).

Calandrino offers Boccaccio the pretext for an exhaustive study of gullibility, including its source in the commitment of one's identity to others. There is an obvious lesson for the reader in this warning about the perils of gullibility, for Bruno and Buffalmacco are both artists—manipulators of illusion at the possible expense of their public. Calandrino personifies the risks that we run by allowing artists to define us as the recipients of their works, and so we must ask if Boccaccio is duping us in any way, making us his Calandrino. On the surface, he is not, for we are privy to the duplicity of Bruno and Buffalmacco, and hence identify more with the tricksters than with their dupe. But if we remember that it was Calandrino's illusion of his own cunning[20] that makes him so susceptible to beguilement, then we will be wary of our own assumption that we know it all, that our *avvedimento* is absolute and flawless, protecting us from any subtler deception on the part of the writer. Calandrino believes that the heliotrope put the secret powers of nature at his disposal, making possible his manipulation of appearances at the service of the perfect crime, and it is this very pretense of cunning which makes him the ideal victim for Bruno and Buffalmacco. Should we assume complete knowledge and *avvedimento*, then we would share in the error of Calandrino and open ourselves to deception by the arch-manipulator of illusion, the writer himself.

Yet Boccaccio has withheld no information pertaining to the machinations of Bruno and Buffalmacco that would make us his dupe. We are thus given the illusion of complete insight into the workings of this tale, and we leave it convinced of our alliance with its

---

[20] Calandrino's pretensions to cunning are well substantiated by Russo, p. 446, and Getto, *Vita di forme*, p. 186. Muscetta sees Calandrino as a newly urbanized country boy eager to embrace his idea of city values, full of get-rich-quick schemes and the illusion of his own cunning. See *Lettura militante*, p. 164.

tricksters, and not with their prey. But the joke on us is a formal one: what we take to be the ending of the story is no ending at all, for the tale of Calandrino will be continued in three installments—VIII, 6, IX, 3, and IX, 5—each of which provides the same illusion of closure. Only in retrospect can we see in the tales such unstable endings that they prove utterly inconclusive. Even the fourth of the Calandrino stories fails to provide finality, for its conclusion is as unstable as the others, and leaves open-ended this potentially limitless sequence of tales, whose resolutions are incomplete because Calandrino is never included in them. He remains trapped in the delusional systems which Bruno and Buffalmacco contrive for him, failing to experience that moment of recognition which would free him from their wiles. Thus, Calandrino never questions the validity of the heliotrope myth in VIII, 3, never learns who stole his pig in VIII, 6, never discovers that he was not pregnant in IX, 3, and never finds out that his beloved is a prostitute and a hypocrite in IX, 5. Since there is no moment of self-recognition for Calandrino in these tales, he cannot learn from his mishaps, and thus remains vulnerable to ever more ludicrous and incredible pranks at the hands of his two painter friends.[21] The protagonist never emerges from his fantasies to see the light of truth, but is simply given a new delusion to replace the last one, and the same basic configuration of events necessarily ensues: Bruno and Buffalmacco want to punish in Calandrino the sin of avarice (VIII, 3, VIII, 6, and IX, 3) or lust (IX, 5); they devise a plan to trap him and arrange all the particulars; Calandrino falls for the bait and is duly punished for the vice of which he remains forever ignorant. By failing to inform Calandrino of the justice of their pranks, Bruno and Buffalmacco allow him to persist in those behaviors and illusions which will invite their continued contrivances.[22]

But we are not aware of the instability and open-endedness of these plots until we have experienced their multiplicity, for only then do we realize that the previous conclusions were incomplete. Our expectations of form are thus doubly thwarted. First, we expect each tale to be discrete and self-sufficient, with beginning, middle, and end. Second,

[21] Other *Decameron* tales have ended with the indefinite perpetuation of a trick, wherein the dupe remains in a permanent state of mystification which the reader projects onto a future of continued deception. But until now, Boccaccio has not seen fit to make *explicit* those future jests by using them as the subject of subsequent stories. Thus, the reader has come to interpret these open-ended conclusions as endings nevertheless, since such narrations will not be continued at a later point in the text. We are therefore not at all prepared for the sudden introduction of a serial mode in the eighth and ninth days, since our reading habits have been so well tested and established after seven days of discrete tales.

[22] On the structural parallelisms of these four tales, see Baratto, *Realtà e stile*, p. 314.

Boccaccio has led us to expect that each story of the *Decameron* will be unique, employing its own *dramatis personae*, and its own interplay of personalities. Indeed, the first seven days of the *Decameron* have admirably confirmed this pattern, setting a trustworthy precedent for subsequent days. But Boccaccio defies our expectations of form by not only violating the law of heterogeneity within the confines of a single day (Day VIII), but also by violating the integrity of the days themselves, for the Calandrino sequence spills over into Day IX.

It is by means of such formal tricks that Boccaccio makes us his dupes, thus locating our gullibility in the rigid and somewhat unconscious expectations we have of literary form. By giving us all the factual information we may need to fully comprehend the narration, Boccaccio fools us into thinking that our cunning matches Bruno's and Buffalmacco's—that we are impervious to deception. But the writer makes us his Calandrino by manipulating narrative form in such a way that we are fooled not once, but three times, into the illusion of finality.

All this would imply that the writer is himself exempt from deception—that he alone, as the ultimate manipulator of illusions, is beyond gullibility. But such an inference fails to take into account the fact that Calandrino is a painter—at once the creator of illusions and their creature.[23] By making this quintessential dupe himself an artist, Boccaccio calls into question his own exemption from gullibility and in so doing denies the privileged status of his perspective. It is just the different degrees of gullibility which distinguish victims and victimizers, for no one within the human order can claim the possession of absolute and unconditional knowledge. Those who make such claims become the greatest of dupes, subject to manipulation by those who accept the relativity and contingency of all human belief. Calandrino's message becomes a secularized version of Ser Ciappelletto's, where gullibility equaled the sin of pride in the presumption of divine understanding. In the world of Calandrino, the pretensions are narrower but the outcome the same: credulity begets its just desserts in pseudo-saints and shattered dreams.[24]

---

[23] Boccaccio's multiplication of internal artist figures is noted by B.J. Layman in "Boccaccio's Paradigm of the Artist." See p. 30 in particular.

[24] For a sensitive and precise analysis of Calandrino's crushed hopes and dreams, see Sapegno, *Il Trecento*, p. 359.

THE MARCHIONESS AND THE DONKEY'S SKULL

THE TALE OF PATIENT GRISELDA (X, 10)

— allegorical readings — Petrarch's 1st of its kind
(Mazzotta, etc.) + the exemplum.
Latin trans.

Up until his final tale, Boccaccio gives us every reason to expect from the tenth and last day of storytelling a conclusion which will satisfy the expectations for closure which Frank Kermode describes in *The Sense of an Ending*. Kermode submits the recurrence of apocalyptic beliefs as evidence for the human preoccupation with finality—a preoccupation which finds fulfillment in "concord fictions" where beginnings and middles make sense in terms of their endings, and conclusions retrospectively order the past in a coherent totality. Those plots will be most satisfying, according to Kermode, which adhere to the paradigm of concord fictions, organizing narrative time in the image of human history as we would want to live it. Thus, we seek assurances of an end which will give significance to duration, alleviating the boredom and despair of undifferentiated temporal succession. If we use Kermode's metaphor of the grandfather clock, our impulse is "to defeat the tendency of the interval between *tick* and *tock* to empty itself, to maintain within that interval following *tick* a lively expectation of *tock*, and a sense that however remote tock may be, all that happens happens as if *tock* were certainly following."[1]

In the final day of storytelling, Boccaccio promises to fulfill these expectations of closure. It is this day which should give form and coherence to the entire work, endowing it with perfection in the etymological sense, and completing the overall comic pattern which critics have found in the progression of daily themes from the squalid or dismal ones of the beginning and middle, to the exalted one of this

---

[1] Frank Kermode, *The Sense of an Ending: Studies in the Theory of Fiction* (New York, 1975), p. 46.

last day,[2] dedicated to "chi liberalmente o vero magnificamente alcuna cosa operasse intorno a' fatti d'amore o d'altra cosa" (635). This triumphant ending should provide a new perspective on the less seemly tales of preceding days, making them necessary prerequisites to this final apotheosis of human nature, rather than absolute commentaries on the decrepitude of mortal existence. That our reading of the entire text should be subject to revision in the light of this last day is suggested by Emilia's admonitory speech to Panfilo, her successor and ruler over this final day's festivities. "Signor mio, gran carico ti resta, sì come è l'avere il mio difetto e degli altri che il luogo hanno tenuto che tu tieni, essendo tu l'ultimo, a emendare" (632). At first glance, this may appear to be a standard expression of the modesty *topos*, but if we look closely at the phrase "il mio difetto e degli altri," we realize that Emilia is commenting on the performance of all the preceding monarchs, and not just on her own. Thus, Panfilo, as the last king of the *Decameron*, is answerable not only for Emilia's excesses in the preceding day, but for the entire course of the storytelling up to the moment of his coronation as ruler of Day X. Emilia could have condensed her phrasing by combining "il mio difetto e degli altri" into the more economical "i nostri difetti." But by separating syntactically these elements, she emphasizes a retrograde movement in time, from Day IX backward through Day I—a movement which will constitute one of the temporal axes of Day X. This regression is countered by an equal and opposite thrust forward as Day X anticipates the time when the pastoral sojourn will be no more, when the *brigata* will have returned to the city, and when we will have completed our reading of this text. The intimation of a future beyond the *Decameron* enters as if by stealth into the introduction to Day X, quietly subverting the ritual certitude of the frame story whose stable patterns of recurrence promised to last forever in a convincing simulacrum of eternity.

It is dawn of the last day, and as the *brigata* sets forth to find a site for telling stories, the conversation takes an unexpected turn. "E molte cose della loro futura vita insieme parlando e dicendo e rispondendo, per lungo spazio s'andaron diportando" (637). This is the first time in the frame story that anything has been said about the world "out there." Pampinea's prohibition against the leakage of bad news into the confines of this pastoral retreat had forestalled any morbid speculation about the fate of the city and its citizens. Assuming that Pampinea's ruling still holds, and judging from the carefree attitude of these youths' "diportando," we may conclude that their musings

---

[2] See Branca, *Boccaccio medievale*, p. 18; Mazzotta, "The Literal and the Allegorical," p. 64; Neri, "Il disegno ideale," p. 54; and Hastings, *Nature and Reason*, pp. 7-9.

are hopeful, if not happy ones, and that this is a promise, on Boccaccio's part, of an overall comic resolution to the frame story itself.

In his choice of subject for Day X, Boccaccio suggests that this is to be a celebration of the entire work and of the art which went into its making. These tales of liberal or magnificent actions exemplify the very virtue which Aristotle likens to art in his *Nichomachean Ethics*. "The magnificent man is like an artist, for he can see what is fitting, and spend large sums tastefully."[3] In the final day of storytelling, the narrators exhibit just those qualities of propriety and taste on which Aristotle bases his comparison, for it is this textual conclusion which gives measure to the whole in the tradition of Aristotelian aesthetics. But there is something else about magnificence which recommends it to Boccaccio's art. "The magnificent man will spend such sums for honor's sake, for this is common to the virtues."[4] Like the magnificent spender, Boccaccio pours out his artistic wealth with no expectation of material return, much to the chagrin of the profit-mongers who cannot sanction anything but the most mercenary motives for human industry. The author answers their arguments in his polemic introduction to the fourth day by ranking poetic riches above material gain in his hierarchy of values. "E già più ne trovarono tralle loro favole i poeti, che molti ricchi tra' loro tesori" (265). Boccaccio strengthens his argument for the primacy of poetic riches over material ones by citing their disparate impact on culture. "E assai già, dietro alle loro favole andando, fecero la loro età fiorire, dove in contrario molti nel cercar d'aver più pane, che bisogno non era loro, perirono acerbi" (265). Poetic riches can be shared by an entire culture, while material wealth diminishes by sharing, and therefore is limited to the individual who is caught in an alternating sequence of desire and gain. There seems to be an ambiguity in the phrase "la loro età," suggesting that poets bring to fruition not only the culture to which they belong, but their own personal lives as well. This latter reading is suggested by the antithesis between the insatiable rich, who die "acerbi," and the poets, who would bring their own lives to maturation in their pursuit of cultural goals. Such ambiguity may be willed on Boccaccio's part if he subscribes to the Aristotelian theory that man can only fully realize his nature in the community of men, making cultural and personal fruition mutually interdependent processes, and ones over which the artist should preside.

---

[3] *The Works of Aristotle*, IX, ed. W.D. Ross (Oxford, 1925), 1122a. That Boccaccio knew the *Ethics* is proved by the existence of a manuscript of the Aristotelian work transcribed and signed by Boccaccio. See Hortis, *Studj sulle opere latine*, pp. 340-341.

[4] *The Works of Aristotle*, IX, 1122b.

This is all by way of proving that the Aristotelian analogy between magnificence and art well suits Boccaccio's own approach to his literary production, which he sees as an outpouring of wealth in the interests of the public good, scorning profit as the motivation for *andando dietro alle favole*. This Aristotelian link entitles us to see Day X, dedicated to magnificent actions, as a meditation on the art which produced this text, and on its lofty and disinterested public purpose. As may well be expected, the tales of this day are peopled with artist figures of various sorts, perverse as well as not, who offer *in bono* and *in malo* examples of the process responsible for the storytelling venture.[5]

Even as he celebrates his art in this concluding day of tales, however, Boccaccio begins to dismantle it by opposing the theme of magnificence to the format which the *brigata* follows in exemplifying that virtue. For the members of the storytelling team are vying with each other in their tales of magnificence as many of the narratives include claims of victory over previous "contenders" and implicit challenges to subsequent tellers to equal or surpass each example.[6] Such a competitive mode subverts the very theme of magnificence, for this virtue suggests the disinterested outpouring of wealth in Dante's sense of celestial economics, where giving increases rather than decreases the donor's assets. Competition implies just the opposite; that is, the increase of one individual's fortunes at the expense of another's, or as Dante describes the earthly marketplace "dove per compagnia parte si scema" (*Purg*. XV, 50). It is striking that this competitive tone occurs only at the end of the text, where it virtually undoes the relaxed, egalitarian mode of the rest of the storytelling venture, characterized as truly magnificent in the generous and disinterested way in which stories had been offered until now. And here, in the very act of celebrating that liberal mode by making magnificence the theme of Day X, Boccaccio subverts it by having his narrators vie with each other in their tales. Storytelling is no longer a selfless attempt to increase the pleasure of the *brigata*, for now the tales have signatures, want trophies, and are dedicated to the glorification of the tellers. The *brigata* is preparing to return to the world "out there." Yet perhaps I exaggerate the importance of this sudden competitive attitude in the context of the *Decameron*, for it indeed conforms to an old *topos* of

[5] See B.J. Layman's "Boccaccio's Paradigm of the Artist" for a study of this theme with particular relevance to Day X.

[6] Three of the tales, X, 2, X, 5, and X, 8, begin with such claims, and three of them, X, 4, X, 5, and X, 8, end thus. Two of the tales, X, 3 and X, 7, though not claiming victory, promise to be no less marvelous than the others. Throughout this day, narrators are comparing their achievements to each other, making previous tales of magnificence explicit measures of their own.

poetic contests in pastoral settings, not to mention the *questioni d'amore* where petitioners argue their case before a queen of love. Though Boccaccio is appropriating a medieval convention, I find it nonetheless significant that he invokes the pastoral contest at this point in his text, as he nears its conclusion and prepares to send the *brigata* back into the savage and possibly lethal city where existence will be predicated on the competitive will to survive.

But the element most disruptive of the nobility and balance of the tenth day is the tale of Griselda—that tale which should retrospectively order the entire text in a coherent totality and complete its overall comic design. Instead, this final story raises many interpretive problems, and calls into question those storytelling norms of the tenth day which had led us to expect a satisfying and triumphant conclusion to the text. Thus, when Boccaccio has his frame story characters quarrel over the meaning of the Griselda tale, he is anticipating the critical controversy which this narrative will spark throughout its long and successful career in European letters.[7] Boccaccio never makes explicit the nature of the *brigata*'s polemic over the tale ("chi d'una parte e chi d'altra tirando, chi biasimando una cosa, un'altra intorno a essa lodandone" 713), leaving it up to each era of readers to assume its own critical positions in the ongoing debate. Ill-at-ease with the literal level of the Griselda story, recent critics fall into two camps: those who make their uneasiness into an interpretive tool, citing the narrator's own internal criticism of the story as the justification for their reading, and those who explain away their uneasiness by construing the literal level as a vehicle for allegorical truths. The first group reads horizontally, seeking meaning in the tension between the narrator's commentary and the tale itself, while the second group moves vertically from literal to allegorical levels of meaning. To the former group belong such critics as Carlo Muscetta, Joy Hambuechen Potter, and Aldo Scaglione, who make much of Dioneo's subversive remarks.[8] Members of the latter group agree that a figural reading explains the anomalies of the tale, but disagree on just what constitutes the allegorical scheme, one seeing in Griselda a *figura Christi*, another a *figura*

---

[7] See Branca, "Origini e fortuna europea della Griselda," in *Boccaccio medievale*, pp. 308-313.

[8] See Muscetta, *Giovanni Boccaccio*, p. 298; Potter, "Boccaccio as Illusionist," pp. 343-344; Scaglione, *Nature and Love*, p. 71; and also Hauvette, *Boccace: Étude biographique*, pp. 301-302. Valency, on the other hand, views modern critical discomfort with the tale of Griselda as a failure of the historical imagination. His reading, however, does not account for the public within the text which also refuses to take Griselda piously. The responses of Dioneo and the quarrelling members of the *brigata* indicate far from the univocal admiration that Valency expects. See *The Palace of Pleasure*, p. 21.

Mariae, and several others the type of Job.[9] Though convincing in themselves, none of these typological readings accounts for Boccaccio's sudden introduction of a figural mode into a text which has been secular up to this point. Why suddenly shift literary registers at the very end of a work which has stubbornly resisted the status of *exemplum*? Not even the medieval convention of the palinode, employed by Dante and Petrarch to renounce their worldly loves for spiritual ones, can satisfactorily explain Boccaccio's apotheosis of Griselda. Petrarch's paean to the Virgin at the end of his *Canzoniere* climaxed 365 poems of vacillation between sacred and profane love, while Dante's purgatorial encounter with Beatrice is the logical fulfillment of his entire poetic past. If Boccaccio's tale of Griselda is to be read as a palinode, more arguments will have to be made for the poetic fitness of such a retraction.

Figural interpretations also fail to explain Dioneo's lubricious remarks at the beginning and the end of the tale. Such a pornographic framework hardly contributes to the solemnity of the spiritual lessons these critics would have us learn. Itala Rutter[10] neatly accounts for Dioneo's perspective in her allegorical reading of the tale by construing the narrator's commentary as an example of that inferior vision which Gualtieri and Griselda transcend in their "higher wisdom" of God's plan. Giuseppe Mazzotta[11] also includes Dioneo's perspective in an interpretation of Boccaccio's allegory. His reading, however, dignifies Dioneo's perspective by seeing in it Boccaccio's critique of the allegorical method.

Studies on the origin of the Griselda story not only help explain the excesses of the plot but give credence to an allegorical interpretation. Dudley Griffith,[12] and later Wirt Armistead Cate[13] argue convincingly that the plot harks back to the Cupid and Psyche type of folk tale in which an other-world creature marries a mortal and subjects the spouse to a series of tests. According to Griffith, Boccaccio's narrative

---

[9] For the Christ analogy, see Marga Cottino-Jones, "Fabula vs. Figura: Another Interpretation of the Griselda Story," in *The Decameron, A New Translation*, ed. Mark Musa and Peter Bondanella (New York, 1977), pp. 295-305. See Branca, *Boccaccio medievale*, pp. 17-18, 97, and 101, for Griselda as a Marian figure. Both Joan Ferrante in "The Frame Characters of the *Decameron*: A Progression of Virtues," *Romance Philology*, 19 (November 1965), 223, and Janet Smarr in "Symmetry and Balance in the *Decameron*," p. 174, find in the Griselda tale analogies to the story of Job.

[10] Itala Tania Rutter, "The Function of Dioneo's Perspective in the Griselda Story," *Comitatus*, 5 (1974), 33-42.

[11] Giuseppe Mazzotta, "The Literal and the Allegorical," pp. 69-70.

[12] Dudley David Griffith, *The Origin of the Griselda Story* (Seattle, 1931).

[13] Wirt Armistead Cate, "The Problem of the Origin of the Griselda Story," *Studies in Philology*, 29 (July 1932), 389-405.

is "at base, a tale of the Cupid and Psyche type and gets its meaning from definitely understood relations between a mortal and an other-world being."[14] This folk origin justifies the lapses in verisimilitude which seem to blight the plot. For example, the fact that Gualtieri descends from a long line of supernatural creatures—monsters, gods in animal disguise, and spell-bound princes—explains his willfulness, his possession of seemingly limitless powers, and his inaccountability to human laws. Griselda's surpassing devotion to this difficult husband can be understood as the intense love inspired by an other-world being in a mortal heart. Many particulars of the Griselda story belong to a subset of the Cupid and Psyche group in which a tabu, or "a requirement placed upon the mortal as a condition of the union"[15] is present. Griselda's promise of absolute obedience to her husband would constitute such a tabu—one which is subjected to the most excruciating tests as the heroine's two infants are taken from her and presumably killed. Griffith proves that this dimension of the plot fits the specifications for a subdivision of the tabu-group in which "children are taken away as a test under the tabu."[16] The Cupid and Psyche type of story usually ends happily as the mortal survives the various trials imposed by the other-world spouse whose doubts about the marriage are finally resolved.

A genetic approach goes far to explain why the Griselda story is so amenable to allegory. Originally drafted to explain the nature of human love for the divine, the story had to adapt itself, through the process called rationalization,[17] to the needs of more sophisticated, less credulous audiences. Accordingly, the other-world creature becomes a nobleman, and the mortal becomes a peasant (shifting the folk tale disparity between superhuman and human into a class difference)[18] so that the original spiritual meaning is displaced from the literal to the allegorical level. Allegory thus becomes a way of maintaining the original supernatural purpose of this folk tale while allowing the narratives to rationalize according to the rules of medieval poetics.

The first critic to give the Griselda story an allegorical reading is, of course, Petrarch, whose Latin translation of Boccaccio's story consti-

---

[14] Griffith, p. 11.
[15] Ibid., p. 31.
[16] Ibid., p. 46.
[17] "This process by which unadaptable or ill-understood details are given a meaning more in accord with contemporary human experience is called rationalization." Ibid., p. 29.
[18] Ibid., pp. 72-73.

tutes a clear statement about the locus of meaning in the tale.[19] Unconvinced by the literal level of events,[20] Petrarch makes this fiction the vehicle of a double didacticism: both secular and religious. The secular moral is the more obvious one, articulated in the very subtitle to the translation: "de Obedientia ac fide uxoria." Again in his concluding remarks, Petrarch insists upon the worldly component of his message by comparing Griselda to a list of exemplars from classical antiquity. Thus, when a friend finds the Griselda story utterly lacking in credibility, Petrarch replies, "who is there who would not, for example, regard a Curtius, a Mucius, or the Decii, among our own people, as pure fictions; or among foreign nations, Codrus and the Philaeni; or since we are speaking of women, Portia, or Hypsicratia, or Alcestis, and others like them? But these are actual historical persons."[21] Thus, Griselda takes her place as a paragon of a pre-Christian morality. More importantly, her marriage exemplifies the intense devotion which should bind the soul to God—an analogy which Petrarch states twice in the epilogue to his translation. Consequently, his purpose in spreading the Griselda story is to encourage readers "to submit themselves to God with the same courage as did this woman to her husband. . . . Anyone, it seems to me, amply deserves to be reckoned among the heroes of mankind who suffer without a murmur for God, what this poor peasant woman bore for her mortal husband."[22] Petrarch has thus made the Boccaccio story an unequivocal pretext for a moral lesson framing his translation with emphatic statements of his didactic purpose. His teaching assumes the status of absolute truth, and therefore no textual element can call into question the authenticity of the *exemplum* nor the authority of his narrative voice. How different is Boccaccio's treatment of the tale, in which the narrator himself casts doubt on both the validity of the moral lesson and the storytelling genre which promises to embody God's truth. For Dioneo's Griselda is embedded in narrative ironies and uncertainties, making her example anything but univocal. This discrepancy between the context and the content of the tale produces the sort of gap which

---

[19] On Petrarch's critique of the *Decameron* and his reasons for translating the Griselda story, see Guiseppe Petronio, "I volti del Decameron," *Boccaccio: Secoli di Vita*, pp. 113-114.

[20] In the epilogue to the translation of the Griselda story which appeared in *Epistolae seniles*, Book XVII, Letter 3, Petrarch writes to Boccaccio: "whether what I have narrated be true or false, I do not know, but the fact that you wrote it would seem sufficient to justify the inference that it is but a tale." The translation is from James Harvey Robinson and Henry Winchester Rolfe, "On Boccaccio's *Decameron* and the Story of Griselda," in *The Decameron*, ed. Musa and Bondanella, p. 186.

[21] Ibid., p. 187.

[22] Ibid., p. 186.

engages the readers' most active participation in an attempt to realign disparate textual elements.[23] The violent critical controversy surrounding Griselda bears witness to the superabundance of such gaps and their appeal to reader activism in the very story which brings the *Decameron* to a close.

The fact that Dioneo is the narrator should arouse readers' suspicions from the start. Throughout the *Decameron*, Dioneo has been the spokesman for the aesthetic of unfettered play. He has been the one to insist on the integrity of the storytelling venture, constructing barriers between the pastoral retreat and the real world's concerns. He is the one to suggest the move to the *Valle delle donne*—the natural setting most remote from the city and most conducive to narrative freedom. When the ladies object to Dioneo's unseemly choice of storytelling topics for Day VII, the king reaffirms the absolute freedom of literary creation by stating, in a roundabout way, the distinction between pornographic speech and pornographic acts.[24] Now Day X threatens the carefully acquired autonomy of this text by reintroducing the genre of the *exemplum* which has been discredited in *Decameron* I, 1. Serving as a model for human conduct, the *exemplum* posits a continuity between the work of art and the world beyond the text, thus violating the entire aesthetic of the *Decameron*, whose stories exist in a space apart from factual reality, told as they are "ne' giardini, in luogo di sollazzo, tra persone giovani" (718).

Nonetheless, when Panfilo announces his intention to dedicate Day X to stories of liberality and magnificence, he implies that the ensuing narratives will have the status of moral *exempla*: "Queste cose e dicendo e faccendo senza alcun dubbio gli animi vostri ben disposti a valorosamente adoperare accenderà: ché la vita nostra, che altro che brieve esser non può nel mortal corpo, si perpetuerà nella laudevole fama" (632). Except for Dioneo, the entire *brigata* responds in kind, with Neifile, Pampinea, and Filomena making explicit their normative intent.[25] So it remains for Dioneo to reassert the integrity of the text

---

[23] This is the thesis of Wolfgang Iser in *The Implied Reader: Patterns of Communication in Prose Fiction from Bunyan to Beckett* (Baltimore, 1974).

[24] Dioneo persuades the ladies that their reluctance to tell off-color stories will convince a suspicious public that they have something to hide. "Chi sapesse che voi vi cessaste da queste ciance ragionare alcuna volta, forse suspicherebbe che voi in ciò foste colpevoli, e per ciò ragionare non ne voleste" (438). Dioneo thus reverses the medieval commonplace that impure deeds follow impure words, and suggests instead the discontinuity between speech and acts.

[25] See the preamble to X, 1 plus the conclusions to X, 7, 8, and 9 for explicit proofs of didacticism on the part of the tellers. (Battaglia, however, sees in the tales of Day X such exaggeration that they reach the very limits of verisimilitude. This excess produces a storytelling mode which fails to attain the status of the *exemplum* because its idiosyncracies defy generalization.) See *Giovanni Boccaccio e la riforma della narrativa*, p. 44.

by separating it off, once and for all, from the tradition of the *exemplum*. Accordingly, he begins his tale by defying his listeners to follow Gualtieri's model. "Vo' ragionar d'un marchese, non cosa magnifica ma una matta bestialità, come che bene ne gli seguisse alla fine; la quale io non consiglio alcun che segua, per ciò che gran peccato fu che a costui ben n'avvenisse" (703). Dioneo's obvious hostility toward his protagonist resurfaces in the conclusion of the story when he begrudges Gualtieri his good fortune: "al quale non sarebbe forse stato male investito d'essersi abbattuto a una che quando, fuor di casa, l'avesse fuori in camiscia cacciata, s'avesse sì a un altro fatto scuotere il pillicione che riuscito ne fosse una bella roba" (712). The levity and nonchalance of this remark should not distract us from its extreme metaliterary importance, for it stands at the end of the storytelling day which itself completes the *Decameron*. What Dioneo has done, then, is to deny closure on several levels, leaving open-ended his tale, the tenth day, and hence the text as a whole.[26] Dioneo's "non-ending" has thus violated all the expectations of form which the grand architectonic design of the *Decameron* had promised, for the 100 (actually 101) tales offered just as many premonitions of an absolute and final end. Each storytelling day had its own conclusion which was a composite of ten smaller ones, and which anticipated the grand finale—itself a composite of ten constituent endings in the ten days of *decameron*. Thus, the very geometric structure of the whole led us to expect ever more fulfilling and inclusive endings which would supersede those on inferior textual levels by a precise factor of ten.

Obviously Dioneo's ending is anything but the culmination of this inexorable movement toward closure. Far from unifying and justifying the preceding text, the teller opens it up to a multiplicity of possible interpretations. By leaving the *brigata* in confusion over the meaning of Dioneo's story, Boccaccio builds into the work his awareness of the problematics of reading. And by refusing the *brigata* any resolution of its debate, Boccaccio suggests the resistance of his text to any one absolute system of interpretation. Thanks to Dioneo, the *Decameron* remains open-ended, irreducible, and fodder for always another book on narrative technique.

But the possibilities of Dioneo's commentary on his tale have yet to be exhausted. In making the transition between the preceding tale and his own, Dioneo refers to still a third story—the tale of Gianni Lotteringhi (VII, 1).[27] "Il buono uomo, che aspettava la seguente

---

[26] On the open-endedness of the *Decameron*, see Mazzotta, "The Literal and the Allegorical," p. 70.

[27] For a rigorous structural analysis of the triangles which emerge from this story, see Cesare Segre, "Funzioni, opposizioni e simmetrie nella Giornata VII del *Decameron*," *Studi sul Boccaccio*, VI (Florence, 1971), 96-97.

notte di fare abbassare la coda ritta della fantasima, avrebbe dati men di due denari di tutte le lode che voi date a messer Torello" (703). This tale about an adulterous wife who invents a witty expedient to pacify both husband and lover, has little to do with either the tale of Griselda, or its predecessor, that of messer Torello. If Dioneo's intent is to inject a note of vulgarity into the pious proceedings of Day X, why allude back to a story told three days and thirty-nine tales ago, when surely more recent allusions would have achieved the same purpose? An analysis of the tale of Gianni Lotteringhi, however, will prove that Dioneo's allusion is by no means an arbitrary one. Like the tale of Griselda, this story calls into question the stability of narrative discourse and the stock conventions of reading.

Monna Tessa, the clever and lusty wife of Gianni Lotteringhi, has been enjoying the secret embraces of Federigo di Neri Pegolotti for quite a while. Since her husband spends most of his time in the city, only occasionally visiting the villa outside Florence where Tessa is lodging for the summer, she has ample opportunity to entertain her lover. However, lest Federigo should pay a call at an inopportune moment, Tessa contrives a sign system to alert her lover of Gianni's arrival. Her device is a donkey's skull mounted on a pole[28] and her signals are two: when the skull faces Florence, Federigo may advance; when it faces Fiesole, he had best keep his distance. One evening, when Tessa plans to dine with her lover, Gianni arrives unexpectedly and Tessa has no time to change her message. Sure enough Federigo knocks on her door that night but Tessa tells her husband that the visitor is a ghost, and through the language of incantation, conveys to Federigo her dilemma:

> Fantasima, fantasima che di notte vai, a coda ritta ci venisti, a coda ritta te n'andrai. Va nell'orto a piè del pesco grosso, troverai unto bisunto e cento cacherelli della gallina mia; pon bocca al fiasco e vatti via, e non far mal né a me né a Gianni mio. (119-450)[29]

Tessa's expedient is a balm to both men's doubts: Federigo need not fear that he has been replaced by another lover, while Gianni is convinced that his wife is an exorcist *in bona fide*. For the purposes of the following discussion, this ending will be labeled Resolution A.

No sooner has the narrator, Emilia, delivered herself of this happy ending than she offers another one in its place, which we will label Resolution B. Seeking to minimize confusion, Emilia only compounds

[28] The donkey's skull has an anthropological as well as a semiotic function in this tale. For its folk tradition as a protective device, see Maurilio Adriani, *Italia magica* (Rome, 1970), p. 249.

[29] See Marga Cottino-Jones, "Magic and Superstition in Boccaccio's *Decameron*," p. 16, for an analysis of the ritual aspects of incantation in this tale.

it by asserting that both endings are accurate, but that Resolution B happened to another man, a certain Gianni di Nello.[30] With this suggestion, the narrator implies the possibility of a new narrative—one with a different protagonist and with a slightly modified ending. Emilia never commits herself to a definitive version of the story, leaving it up to her readers to choose among the following alternatives:

1. Tale of Gianni Lotteringhi with Resolution A
2. Tale of Gianni Lotteringhi with Resolution B
3. Tale of Gianni Lotteringhi with Resolution A
   Tale of Gianni di Nello with Resolution B

For the logic of Emilia's multiple endings, we do well to study the text of Resolution B. It is here that a theory of language emerges which explains this story's susceptibility to change. According to Resolution B, Tessa knows of her husband's arrival and therefore turns the donkey's skull towards Fiesole. Her signal, however, is accidentally altered by a worker who takes a playful swipe at the donkey's skull and sends it spinning. When the skull comes to rest, it is pointing towards Florence—a signal which Federigo interprets as an invitation to spend the night. Tessa delivers an incantation different from the one in Resolution A, for now she must explain how her message got confused: "Fantasima, fantasima, fatti con Dio, ché la testa dell'asino non vols'io, ma altri fu, che tristo il faccia Iddio, e io son qui con Gianni mio" (450). Resolution B is thus about the instability of language and its openness to misinterpretation.[31] The position of the donkey's skull is a linguistic sign whose significatory function can be disrupted by the forces of accident and chance: a worker's caprice or a strong gust of wind. Language and linguistic constructs are thus presented as anything but absolute, subject as they are to all kinds of external forces beyond the control of the writer. The instability of the linguistic construct, as revealed by the sign of the donkey's skull, is reflected on the formal level by Emilia's insistence that her tale is really an item of gossip—the most untrustworthy of human utterances. Though this may be another example of Boccaccio's self-deprecatory wit, it also

[30] Giuseppe Billanovich finds in this alternative ending a sly dig at a Florentine compatriot. Gianni di Nello was a pharmacist who died in 1347 and was buried in Santa Maria Novella. Boccaccio's malice, according to Billanovich, is in having Emilia tell the tale, for Gianni's wife was one Emiliana—giving the alternate ending an autobiographic sting on the storyteller's part. See *Restauri boccacceschi* (Rome, 1945), pp. 112-119.

[31] Only after having written this chapter did I gain access to Franco Fido's essay "Rhetoric and Semantics in the *Decameron*," *Yale Italian Studies*, 2 (Winter 1978), whose discussion of the semiotics of the donkey's skull and the implications of multiple endings is, at points, similar to my own. See, in particular, his pp. 8-9.

testifies to the highly subjective, fluctuating quality of literary discourse. By reducing his storytelling to the level of hearsay, Boccaccio again discourages us from giving unequivocal authority to his narrative voice. His text comprises just one element in the chain of gossip, each link of which modifies and distorts stories like so many swipes at the donkey's skull.

Dioneo's allusion to the tale of Gianni Lotteringhi in the preface to *Decameron* X, 10 is thus by no means haphazard. If the lessons of the earlier tale are to be applied to that of Griselda, we must remember that no interpretation is absolute, that the linguistic sign is susceptible to infinite distortion and misunderstanding, and therefore that no version of a tale is final. Now it is clear why Boccaccio leaves the *brigata* in dispute over the Griselda story. As internalized readers of the text, the last critical act which the *brigata* members perform upholds the multiplicity and relativity of literary interpretation. Nor is their critical discord presented as cause for alarm—it does not even ruffle the calm and peace of the frame story, which moves inexorably towards its comic resolution.

The Griselda tale may then be read as the most extreme argument for the need to entertain several, possibly contradictory, perspectives at once. The fact that Dioneo vociferously disagrees with his own story is immediate evidence of Boccaccio's pluralism. If we read this tale as a lesson in reading, then several aspects of the narration gain new importance. First, we notice the conspicuous presence of an internal public which acts like a dramatic chorus, witnessing and commenting on every significant narrative development.[32] It is this public which sets the story in motion by urging the marquess of Saluzzo to marry and produce an heir. Gualtieri predicates his decision to wed on two conditions, each of which underlines the significance of the public and his power over it. First, he must be free to choose a spouse with no interference from his subjects and, second, they must agree to honor whomever he should so select. Like nearly every event in this story, Gualtieri's initial meeting with Griselda is a public event, and before she has the chance to recover from the shock of his proposal, she is publicly disrobed, publicly dressed, and publicly married. The townsfolk of Saluzzo thus perform an important collective role in the story and when they are won over to Griselda's side after originally opposing the marquess' low marriage, their response is a normative one. Gualtieri falsifies this consensus and uses it as the excuse for his savage trials of Griselda as he successively seizes and presumably puts

---

[32] In fact, Nino Borsellino cites the Griselda tale, among others, to prove the fundamentally theatrical nature of the collection. See "*Decameron* come teatro," p. 22.

to death her two infants, claiming that his subjects will not brook an heir from such humble stock. Thus, the very force which motivated him to seek a wife is perverted by Gualtieri into the reason for her ordeals. When the marquess informs Griselda of his plans to divorce her and marry another, this interview takes place in public and occasions the melodramatic debate over how the lady should dress (if at all) for her departure from the household. Gualtieri is the target of further criticism, this time on the part of the ladies-in-waiting, when he allows his former wife to appear in public meanly dressed in her capacity as head domestic for the wedding festivities. This choral censorship of Gualtieri's acts echoes our own sense of outrage at the marquess' insatiable need to humiliate his lady. Of course, the recognition scene is staged publicly, as is Gualtieri's announcement of his benign didactic intent in torturing Griselda. The trials, he explains, have had instruction as their purpose: to teach Griselda how to be a good wife, and his subjects how to choose one. Accountability to the public thus becomes the pretext for all Gualtieri's actions, from marrying Griselda to cruelly testing her for fourteen years.

If the people of Saluzzo constitute an internal reading public, offering a critical response to the tale as intimate witnesses of its action, then Gualtieri functions as the figure of the artist who manipulates the tale of Griselda as if from above. Several critics concur with evidence gathered from the folk origin of the tale that Gualtieri acts the role of a God, ordering Griselda's trials "a antiveduto fine" (711) in a parody of providential history.[33] Gualtieri's particular mimesis of the deity would thus take the form of the *deus artifex* in keeping with his aesthetic function as the author of Griselda's story. The marquess is quite literally the creator of Griselda, as Marga Cottino-Jones observes, calling the character into being when he summons her at the well (for this is the first time we hear her name) and bestowing upon his bride the luxury and ease which will allow her to blossom.[34] It is not enough, however, for him merely to bring such a creature into being. His power over her must be continuously validated, even if such proofs lead him to the paradoxical extreme of destroying his creature. The entire story is thus a testing of these creative powers, placing Gualtieri in the ranks of the artist figures who populate the tales of Day X.

If Gualtieri's subjects are readers of his fiction, we may ask what makes their reading distinctive. Above all, they are literal-minded,

---

[33] For example, see Rutter, "The Function of Dioneo's Perspective," p. 37; Cottino-Jones, "Fabula vs. Figura," pp. 298-299; and Mazzotta, "The Literal and the Allegorical," p. 66.

[34] Cottino-Jones, "Fabula vs. Figura," pp. 299-300.

taking their lord at his word when he promises to murder his two children and divorce his wife. Their proximity to the events and their consequent lack of critical distance make this audience an inconstant one, changing its opinion of their lord with his every caprice. The public shifts from dissatisfaction with Gualtieri to satisfaction with him three times during the course of the narration: when he agrees to marry, when his low-born bride proves herself a lady at heart, and when Gualtieri ends his sadistic career as a wife-tester. Dioneo sums these multiple shifts of sympathies in the observation: "e savissimo reputaron Gualtieri, come che troppo reputassero agre e intollerabili l'esperienze prese della sua donna" (712). This public response parallels the trajectory of medieval comedy, "a tristibus incipit sed cum letis desinit."[35]

Whether or not they approve of Gualtieri's actions, his constituents invariably acquiesce to their lord's will. Gualtieri thus enjoys the enviable, if dangerous, role of the fiction-maker whose public imposes no limits on the exercise of his creative powers. Such is not the case with Dioneo, however, whose audience is a jury of peers, themselves practitioners of the storyteller's art, and by now well versed in its ruses. The fact that listeners alternate as tellers in the *brigata* thus ensures that no narrator can lay claim to absolute authority and that storytelling norms will be held up to constant and thorough scrutiny.

Then what about Boccaccio—will he adhere to Gualtieri's example, or to Dioneo's? As the sole author, Boccaccio could appropriate the model of the feudal lord, authoritarian purveyor of the narrative word. Yet he refuses to do so, for Boccaccio, like Dioneo, realizes that he is a storyteller among storytellers—that his book is simply one moment in a continuous tradition of tale-bearing. As he puts his own personal stamp on the narratives which he inherited, so others will modify and distort his legacy. Perhaps the best analogue for Boccaccio's storytelling function is that of the gossip, like Emilia's source for the tale of Gianni Lotteringhi who gives credence to several versions of a tale by simply changing a name. The arbitrariness and fluidity of storytelling makes this text as unstable as the donkey's skull which, with one playful swipe, can come to mean something entirely different.

As critics of their own stories, the members of the *brigata* have come a long way since the opening tale of the *Decameron*. At the outset, Boccaccio had placed an ironic distance between this internal public and his readers by making Panfilo, the narrator of *Decameron* I, 1 a

---

[35] Uguccione da Pisa, *Derivationes* excerpted in Pio Rajna, "Il titolo del poema dantesco," *Studi danteschi*, IV (1921), 26.

misreader of his own tale and having the *brigata* follow his example. Panfilo erred in trying to make an *exemplum* out of a story which resisted his pious exegesis. In the Griselda story, Dioneo does just the opposite by denying the didacticism of a tale which demands to be read as an *exemplum*. The first and last stories of the *Decameron* thus reverse the relationships between tellers' commentary and the narrative itself. However, the ironic distance that had originally separated readers from the internal public has diminished to nothing as we concur with the frame story youths in their confusion over the meaning of the final tale. The *brigata*'s ambivalence is not something which we smile at from the perspective of a superior knowledge, it is something we actively share in as the most honest reaction to the text whose multiplicity defies any reductive systems of interpretation.

The Griselda story offers perhaps the best argument for the allegory of form. The metaliterary importance of this tale does not emerge from a study of content alone. The story line, with its dramatic excesses and its lapses in verisimilitude is so unsatisfying that it has sent many readers on a quest for meaning on an allegorical level. But, as Mazzotta suggests, this too yields an imperfect reading.[36] Only by considering its formal context, i.e., the teller's commentary, the various internal publics, and the terminal position of the tale in the sequence of stories, can we begin to do justice to its meaning. What Ser Ciappelletto told us in prospect, Griselda tells us in retrospect: that no interpretation is final and that critics must be open to ever more inclusive, never conclusive readings.

In his refusal to be didactic at this point in the text, Boccaccio's own special form of didacticism emerges.[37] Unlike Dante, whose teachings are univocal and direct, residing in the content of the work, Boccaccio makes his points through subtle manipulations of form, leaving it up to the readers to discern his moral lesson. Thus, when he argues for the subjectivity of the reading experience in the conclusion to his *Decameron*, Boccaccio is not only protecting the work from charges of indecency, but also reaffirming the public's role in determining textual meaning. "Niuna corrotta mente intese mai sanamente parola: e così come le oneste a quella non giovano, così quelle che tanto oneste non sono la ben disposta non posson contaminare" (718), he writes, displacing the didactic power of the word from the printed page to the mind of the reader. Indeed, nowhere is the public's responsibility made more obvious than in the final tale, as the author denies the possibility of closure and refuses to privilege any one interpretation

---

[36] See Mazzotta, "The Literal and the Allegorical," pp. 67-68.
[37] On Boccaccio's indirect didacticism, see R. Hastings, *Nature and Reason*, p. 6.

over all others. By now, Boccaccio deems his readers expert enough to determine for themselves the meaning of a text which remains so provocatively inconclusive. What constitutes their education in reading? The ability to entertain a plurality of perspectives, the understanding that significance inheres not in the content of a work alone, but also in the various aspects of its form, the knowledge that literary discourse is as unstable as a donkey's skull mounted on a stick, and that what matters for Boccaccio is not where the donkey's skull points, but how easily it can be set spinning.

EPILOGUE

THE CONSOLATION OF STORYTELLING

Allusions to the work of Dante have punctuated these pages: his didacticism, his definitions of novelty, fortune and old age, his damning example of Paolo and Francesca, and his consequent notion of the book as Galeotto. And yet, it was my contention at the outset that critics err in reading Boccaccio with Dante in mind—that this bias produces a skewed and unreasonable portrait of the writer as devoid of all moral concerns. The burden of the preceding pages has been, instead, to reveal Boccaccio's interest in the normative power of the word and in the resulting uses and abuses of literary creation. Though different from Dante's, his is nonetheless a persuasive and coherent morality whose most effective vehicle is the *Decameron* itself. Before closing, then, it behooves us to consider the question of literary influence (by this I do not intend the study of sources)[1] and finding in Dante an inadequate model, to look elsewhere for an analogue to Boccaccio's moral vision.[2]

This is not to deny Boccaccio's reverence for the author of the *Commedia*, nor his intimate knowledge of the older poet's achievement. Homages to Dante abound in Boccaccio's writings, from flagrant borrowings in his early works[3] to his biography of the poet, called in fact a book of praise—*Trattatello in laude di Dante*—which enjoyed such success that it inspired an entire literary genre.[4] Dante served

---

[1] For this, the reader is referred to A.C. Lee, *The 'Decameron': Its Sources and Analogues* (New York, 1966).

[2] In his essay "Dante personaggio mancato del *Decameron*," Franco Fido explains why the earlier poet cannot provide a model for Boccaccio's moral vision. Exploring various levels of Dantesque borrowings in the *Decameron*, Fido shows how Boccaccio systematically evades or undoes Dante's moral judgments.

[3] Carlo Grabher, "Il culto del Boccaccio per Dante e alcuni aspetti delle sue opere dantesche," *Studi danteschi*, 30 (1951), 131.

[4] Pier Giorgio Ricci, "Dante e Boccaccio," *Alighieri*, 16, i-ii (1975), 75.

not only as an inspiration for Boccaccio's own fiction-making, but as a literary study in his own right. A devoted student of the *Commedia*, Boccaccio copied it at least three times[5] and glossed it in his *Esposizioni sopra la Comedia di Dante*. Though never completed, this commentary on the first seventeen cantos of *Inferno* reveals Boccaccio's twofold relationship to the poet: Dante is at once *auctoritas*, deserving an exegesis worthy of Holy Writ; and colleague, inviting the aesthetic judgments of a fellow poet.[6] It is not my place here to rehearse the critical tradition which surrounds the relationship Boccaccio-Dante, whose bibliography, as Aldo Rossi complains, is at least "elefantiaca,"[7] but to suggest the way in which the *Decameron* constitutes a rejection of the Dantesque model in Boccaccio's quest for one more suited to his ideological and aesthetic needs.

One of the most profound ways in which Boccaccio distances himself from his predecessor is through a linguistic relativism which would be anathema to Dante, for whom "the immutable order of things created must be paralleled and mirrored by that of signs."[8] The earlier poet would never abide the unstable language of a Boccaccio who gives characters multiple, interchangeable names (Cipolla's Guccio [VI, 10]) and gives multiple, mutually exclusive endings to his stories (Gianni Lotteringhi [VII, 1] and Griselda [X, 10]). This difference widens the poetic gap between Dante and Boccaccio into a virtual chasm: for Dante, the human word can, under the proper aegis, point beyond itself to transcendent meaning, whereas Boccaccio seriously questions man's pretensions to divine truth and warns continually about the dangers of absolute faith in human utterance.

It was De Sanctis who first applied the fortunate label "commedia umana" to the *Decameron*,[9] vindicating the autonomy of the text while betraying the inevitable critical tendency to measure it against Dante's masterwork. Boccaccio himself invites this dual approach in the opening passage of his introduction by comparing his plague chronicle to a mountain whose ascent will be rewarded by a sojourn in a *locus amoenus* atop purgatorial heights.

> Questo orrido cominciamento vi fia non altramenti che a' camminanti una montagna aspra e erta, presso alla quale un bellissimo piano e dilettevole sia reposto, il quale tanto più viene lor piacevole quanto maggiore è stata del salire e dello smontare la gravezza. (9)

[5]   Ibid., pp. 78-79.
[6]   Grabher, "Il culto del Boccaccio," p. 135.
[7]   Aldo Rossi, "Dante nella prospettiva del Boccaccio," *Studi danteschi*, 37 (1960), 139.
[8]   Franco Fido, "Boccaccio's *Ars Narrandi* in the Sixth Day of the *Decameron*," p. 236.
[9]   See *Storia della letteratura italiana*, p. 297. Soon after, Carducci was to elaborate on this phrase in his critical study *Petrarca e Boccaccio, edizione nazionale delle opere di Giosuè Carducci*, XI (Bologna, 1962), 326-327.

This passage suggests the pastoral nature of Boccaccio's venture, and sets him at odds with the Dantesque model of spiritual pilgrimage—a model which Boccaccio invokes in the words *aspra* and *erta* of *Inferno* I, and in the likeness of his landscape to the topography of Purgatory. Yet this physical similarity conceals a vast difference in announced moral purpose. Where Dante celebrates the harshness of the landscape, and insists on the transience of the pilgrim's sojourn in Eden, Boccaccio apologizes for the ascent and promises indefinite repose in the garden.[10] The storyteller predicates his art on the very leisure that Dante abhors. According to both Charles Singleton and Guiseppe Mazzotta,[11] Boccaccio revels in the aesthetic abstraction from moral care that Cato punishes in Dante when he sends the pilgrim scurrying up the difficult slopes of *Purgatory* II. It is here, then that Boccaccio announces his radical departure from Dantesque influence and initiates a quest for another model, both author and text, which will give his narratives a moral justification without subordinating them to a rigid didacticism. That model, I believe, is Boethius, and that text, his *Consolatio philosophiae*.[12]

*

*   *

As H.R. Patch argues,[13] the impact of Boethius on medieval thought was inestimable. Not only was he popularly regarded as a saint,[14] but his works on logic, arithmetic, geometry, music, as-

---

[10] Accordingly, Padoan finds Boccaccio's reading of Dante superficial and uncommitted. See "Mondo aristocratico e mondo communale," pp. 124-125. Hence, Hauvette finds the *Decameron* "la négation, ou plutôt la dérision" of the *Commedia* in a sphere "manifestement très inférieure à celle de Dante." See *Boccace: Étude biographique et littéraire*, pp. 278-279.

[11] Singleton, "On Meaning in the *Decameron*," p. 119; Mazzotta, "The Literal and the Allegorical," p. 56.

[12] For a theory of imitation which may explain, in a general sense, Boccaccio's preference for a classical over a medieval model, see Harry Berger, "L.B. Alberti on Painting: Art and Actuality in Humanist Perspective," *The Centennial Review*, 10 (1966), especially pp. 266-277. Of the critics who have made passing comments on the occurrence of Boethian thought in Boccaccio, none has pursued a systematic study of this influence on the *Decameron*. See, for example, Cioffari, "The Concept of Fortune in the *Decameron*," pp. 134, 135; Branca, *Boccaccio medievale*, pp. xii, 16, 48; and Hortis, *Studj sulle opere latine del Boccaccio*, pp. 473-475. Hollander sees a substantial debt to Boethius in the framing situation of the *Corbaccio* which depends on the notion of consolation. See *Boccaccio's Two Venuses*, pp. 22-23. Other minor works in which Boethian thought is conspicuous include the *Amorosa visione*, especially Cantos XXXI-XXXVIII, and the *De casibus virorum illustrium*.

[13] See *The Tradition of Boethius* (New York, 1935).

[14] D.W. Robertson, *A Preface to Chaucer: Studies in Medieval Perspectives* (Princeton, 1973), p. 472.

tronomy, and philosophy constituted the very foundation of both the trivium and the quadrivium, and hence of the medieval educational system as a whole.[15] Of all his treatises, however, the *Consolatio* was the one which would enshrine Boethian thought for centuries to come. Countless translations were to attend this document throughout its medieval career (Chaucer's among them),[16] while titles alone betray the many imitations which Boethius inspired throughout Europe, from the twelfth-century *Consolatio morte amici* by Lawrence of Durham to the influential thirteenth-century *Consolatio theologiae* by Johannes of Dambach.[17] The tremendous popularity of this text in the Middle Ages, and the abundance of manuscripts in circulation leave no question as to the accessibility of the *Consolatio* to Boccaccio. The presence of direct allusions to Boethius, and the demonstration, on several occasions, of a profound understanding of his philosophical text suggest that Boccaccio's knowledge of the Latin work was by no means second hand. It is my aim here to show how adroitly the medieval storyteller has used Boethian thought to give dignity and philosophical legitimacy to his narrative venture. Let me qualify this claim by stating the obvious: the *Consolatio* does not serve as a model in any programmatic way, for the external differences between the two works are momentous. The *Decameron* is not written in prosimetrum, it is not an interior monologue or dream vision, there is no guide in allegorical dress, nor is it a justification of the ways of God to man. Yet in the governing idea of the *Decameron* Boccaccio owes a considerable debt to his Boethian model, and it is the *De genealogia* which will allow us to forge a link between the sixth-century philosophical treatise and the collection of tales written some 800 years later.

Boccaccio invites us to consider his debt to Boethius early in the *Decameron*. The author's proemial statement of narrative intent leans heavily on the notion of consolation when he expresses gratitude to a friend whose "piacevoli ragionamenti" saved him from the supreme anguish of unrequited love. Boccaccio never reveals the content of this therapeutic discourse, but goes on to say that he in turn plans to comfort fellow sufferers in love with stories. The suggestion is that the unspecified "piacevoli ragionamenti" are themselves stories, and the unnamed friend the spokesman for the storytelling legacy to which

[15] See Patch, *The Tradition of Boethius*, pp. 33-39.
[16] For a description of Chaucer's translation of the *Consolatio* and a passing account of its impact on some of Chaucer's other work, see Patch, pp. 66-73. An eloquent example of the insights gained by a study of Chaucer's application of Boethian themes may be seen in James Wimsatt's "Medieval and Modern in Chaucer's *Troilus and Criseyde*," *PMLA*, 92 (March 1977), 209-210.
[17] Patch, p. 92.

Boccaccio is heir. The *Decameron* will thus take its place in the cumulative tradition of consolation through fiction, passing on to future readers the solace of these tales, as they were received from a prior source. Though Boccaccio's expression of thanks to his friend has a characteristically melodramatic tinge ("Nella qual noia tanto rifrigerio già mi porsero i piacevoli ragionamenti d'alcuno amico e le sue laudevoli consolazioni, che io porto fermissima opinione per quelle essere avvenuto che io non sia morto" 3), it should be noted that *aegritudo amoris* was a highly documented medical syndrome whose terminal effects were taken quite seriously by medieval scientists as well as by victims of unrequited passion.[18] That Boccaccio was literally saved from the clutches of death by a storytelling friend must therefore not be read as hyperbole, but as a creditable statement of the healing powers of fictions. It is thus in the proem that Boccaccio establishes the theme of consolation by storytelling and alerts us to the Boethian subcurrent which will enrich and ennoble his narrative venture.

The author's personal experience of remedial fictions is reflected on another textual level by the example of the frame story youths who flee the death-dealing city for a storytelling sojourn in the hills of Settignano. Here, the *aegritudo amoris* of the proem is replaced by the indiscriminate destruction of the Black Death, but the remedy is the same in both cases, regardless of the etiology or magnitude of disease: storytelling. By positing the therapeutic effects of fiction-making, Boccaccio locates himself in a long and robust narrative tradition: stories were told to stave off death, as in the *Thousand and One Nights*, to buy time, as in *Ardji Bardji* and the *Contes du perroquet*, to prolong the interval between the intent to act and its completion.[19] In accordance with this tradition, the *brigata*'s decision to leave the pestilential city and to tell tales makes storytelling tantamount to a redemption from death.

The theme of consolation gains enormous force when applied to this life-sustaining activity, and it is here that Boccaccio realizes his Boethian inheritance to the fullest. Boethius takes consolation to mean not merely the alleviation of psychic pain, but the sustenance of life in its highest sense. The philosopher thus transcends the narrow classical concept of consolatory oratory—a subheading of epideictic

[18] See, for example, Massimo Ciavolella, "La tradizione dell'*aegritudo amoris* nel *Decameron*," *Giornale storico della letteratura italiana*, 147 (1970), 496-517; John Livingston Lowes, "The Loveres Maladye of Hereos," *Modern Philology*, 11 (1913-1914), 490-547; and Robertson, *A Preface to Chaucer*, pp. 108-110.

[19] V. Šklovsky, "La construction de la nouvelle et du roman," *Théorie de la littérature: Textes des formalistes russes*, ed. Tzvetan Todorov (Paris, 1965), p. 189.

oratory which confines itself to formulaic expressions of mourner's grief.[20] The *Consolatio* is, instead, a testament to the eternal life of the soul when freed from the accidents of external fortune and the threat of physical extinction. In Books I and II, Lady Philosophy discredits the importance of external goods which offer only the most illusory happiness and subject their possessors to inevitable disappointment. Book III espouses the ideal of spiritual self-sufficiency, poetically restating its arguments in the splendid verses which begin:

> The man who searches deeply for the truth, and wishes to avoid being deceived by false leads, must turn the light of his inner vision upon himself. He must guide his soaring thoughts back again and teach his spirit that it possesses hidden among its own treasures whatever it seeks outside itself.[21]

Book IV argues for an ordered cosmos despite the disparate evidence of injustice in worldly affairs, and Book V reconciles the notions of free will and divine foreknowledge in the most difficult and theologically important passages of the entire text.

Boccaccio obviously does not make his narratives the vehicles for metaphysical speculations on the origin of world order, the status of evil, and the place of free will in a divinely ordained cosmos. He stops short of these considerations and remains at the level of the humanly observable, without contemplating what lies beyond. But this is not to suggest an absence of moral concerns. Within the human order, Boccaccio argues that men take responsibility for their actions and their choices—that, within the limits of certain material and social constraints, humans have the power to affect their destinies. Cisti the baker (VI, 2) may be a member of the working class, but his wit is not without impact on his social superiors. Andreuccio (II, 5) may have been subjected to an unusually large dose of misfortune, but he learns to roll with the punches and ultimately to administer some of his own. Madonna Filippa (VI, 7) may be caught in the commission of a capital crime, but she manages to escape the death sentence by devising a witty defense in court.[22] Melchisedech (I, 3) may be a member of a persecuted race and thus a doubly powerless subject of the sultan, but

---

[20] See Ernst Curtius, *European Literature and the Latin Middle Ages*, trans. Willard R. Trask (New York and Evanston, 1963), pp. 80-82.

[21] Boethius, *The Consolation of Philosophy*, trans. Richard Green (Indianapolis and New York, 1962), p. 69. Unless otherwise noted, all quotations and allusions to the *Consolatio* will be from this translation, and the page numbers will be included in the body of the text.

[22] Kenneth Pennington shows how the protagonist's defense is predicated on two medieval commonplaces: a legal maxim and a Scriptural allusion. See "A Note to *Decameron* VI, 7: The Wit of Madonna Filippa," *Speculum*, 52 (October 1977), 902-905.

through wit he is able to transform persecution into admiration, hostility into friendship. The *Decameron* is a manifesto of human resourcefulness, militating against any notion of a determinism which would allow men to displace responsibility for their lives onto superhuman forces.[23] Boccaccio's stories then exemplify the results of Boethius' climactic meditation on free will and divine foreknowledge. By ending his *Consolatio* with an affirmation of the doctrine of free will in a universe whose events are nonetheless completely known to God, Boethius is making a final plea for moral responsibility. This challenge is admirably met by Boccaccio in his stories of human efficacy in the face of external dangers and threats.

But in his treatise, Boethius isolates another kind of consolation—a false consolation which Lady Philosophy must correct. This is the kind of comfort which intensifies the self-pity of the sufferer, celebrating his pain in the act of soothing it. When Lady Philosophy enters the prison cell of Boethius, she must chase away the Muses who are stationed at his bedside, offering their illusory consolation. "When she saw the Muses of poetry standing beside my bed and consoling me with their words, she was momentarily upset and glared at them with burning eyes" (4).[24] The distressed lady uses harsh language to dismiss her rivals. "Get out, you Sirens, your sweetness leads to death. Leave him to be cured and made strong by my Muses" (5). The false consolation of these Sirens is lethal, while the consolation of Philosophy will be life-sustaining. What these seductive ladies do to make Philosophy so angry is never made explicit, but if we read between the lines, we find them enticing Boethius to despair. The first poem in the volume, recited under their fatal auspices, is a testament to self-pity. Boethius rehearses his misfortunes, and sees no way out of his wretched state of mind. It is his obsession with worldly disappointments which Lady Philosophy must replace with a new attitude of self-sufficiency and inner peace.

The two diametrically opposed meanings of consolation embodied by the debilitating Muses, and by Lady Philosophy, are central to Boethian thought. The superficial consolation which appeals to the senses and binds man to his mortality must be overcome by a deeper, more satisfying consolation which transcends the limits of the sublu-

---

[23] Boccaccio's contempt for such moral abdication is made explicit in his *Esposizioni sopra la Comedia di Dante*, p. 401, as he glosses Virgil's answer to Dante on the theological status of Fortuna in Canto VII.

[24] The original Latin, however, does not explicitly mention consolation. "Quae ubi poeticas Musas vidit, nostro assistentes toro, fletibusque meis verba dictantes, commota paulisper, ac torvis inflammata luminibus." *De consolatione philosophiae* (London, 1823), pp. 67-68.

nary world. But the experience of false consolation is a necessary first step in the ascent to true spiritual self-sufficiency. Without this consolation *in malo*, the appreciation of true consolation would not be possible. "Just so, by first recognizing false goods, you begin to escape the burden of their influence; then afterwards, true goods may gain possession of your spirit" (43). This parallels the traditional Christian notion of conversion which presupposes a descent into error as a prelude to the embrace of truth.

For Petrarch, the Boethian distinction between two types of Muses and hence two types of poetic consolation becomes a handy weapon against those who use Boethius as cannon fodder for their antihumanism. In his *Invectivae contra medicum*, written around 1352, Petrarch answers his adversary by citing the opening pages of the *Consolatio* in which the ailing prisoner entertains the sluttish Muse who is soon to be banished from his bedside:

> Certainly if you had understood any of those things about which you discourse so thoughtlessly, you would know that the woman of the theater [the sluttish Muse] whom Boethius mentions is not held in esteem by the poets themselves. Moreover, you did not see, blind one, what followed, although you ignorantly put the passage itself in your letter. What does she [Lady Philosophy] say, in fact? "Let him be cured and made well by the true Muses." These are the Muses in whom the poets (if any still exist anywhere today) glory and trust, with whose help they have learned not to slaughter the physically sick, but to succour the sick of mind.[25]

Of considerable interest in Petrarch's argument is his appropriation of a recurrent Boethian theme: that of disease. Lady Philosophy again and again refers to the prisoner's wrong-headedness as an illness amenable only to philosophical cure. It is especially fitting that Petrarch avail himself of this theme in view of his adversary, who is a nameless physician. The man of letters is thereby able to take the offensive, transforming his opponent's attack on poetry as impractical[26] into a critique of the physician's own practical incompetence by implying that medical men, unlike poets, do slaughter the physically sick.

---

[25] *Opere latine di Francesco Petrarca*, ed. Antonietta Bufano (Turin, 1975). The English translation of this passage is mine. The Latin passage reads as follows: "Certe siquid eorum de quibus tam temerarie disputas didicisses, scires scenicam illam quam Boetius notat, ipsos inter poetas in precio non haberi. Non autem vidisti, cece, quod iuxta erat, licet id ipsum literis tuis ignoranter insereres. Quid enim ait? 'Veris eum Musis curandum sanandumque relinquite.' Hee sunt Muse quibus, si qui usquam hodie supersunt, poete gloriantur ac fidunt, quarum ope non egra corpora mactare, sed egris animis succurrere didicerunt" (840-842).

[26] Petrarch's unnamed adversary has criticized poetry as "unnecessary." See Book III of the *Invectivae contra medicum*, pp. 895ff.

Boccaccio offers a more ample treatment of the Boethian distinction between good and bad Muses in the passionate apology, written
during the 1360's, which climaxes his *De genealogia*. It is in Book xiv,
section 20, that Boccaccio displays an intimate knowledge not only of
Boethian thought, but of the text which immortalized it. Boccaccio
strategically cites the *Consolatio* to support his own defense of poetry,
and as Petrarch has done before him, rescues Boethius from the
hands of the poet-haters, who had used his text to support their
position. These philistines had read Lady Philosophy's dismissal of
the Muses from Boethius' bedside as a symbolic rejection of all poetry.
"Little do they understand Boethius' words: they consider them super-
ficially, wherefore they bawl at the gentle and modest Muses."[27] But
Boccaccio, along with Petrarch, shows how the poet-haters had taken
Lady Philosophy's arguments out of context and had grievously mis-
represented the author's intent. They neglect the fact that Lady
Philosophy dismisses the false Muses so that she may usher in her
own, and so replace these pseudo-consolers with the Muses of true
consolation. This distinction is of crucial importance to Boccaccio,
who uses it as the basis for his defense of poetry. "There are two kinds
of poets: one worthy of praise and reverence, always acceptable to
good men, the other obscene and detestable, who, I said, should be
both expelled and exterminated."[28] Boccaccio answers the Platonists,
who reject all art as self-serving illusion, with a second kind of art—
that which adorns philosophical truths and entices men to their pursuit. He observes Boethius' persistent use of these second Muses to
embellish Lady Philosophy's teachings. "And, by way of clearer proof
that he was talking of the second sort of Muses, Philosophy later cites
many a fragment of verse and poetic fable to soothe and console
Boethius. So if these good Muses have a share in the healing art of
Philosophy, they must be reputable perforce."[29]

Both Petrarch and Boccaccio abide by the Boethian identification of
the bad Muses as those of the theater—the *meretriculae scenicae*[30] who
act out indecencies and tempt their audiences into similar practices.
According to Boccaccio, the comic dramatists, and these alone, are the
targets of Plato's attack on poets,[31] as well as Boethius', and he numbers among those so charged the Ovid of the *Ars amatoria*. This is all
very puzzling for the reader who wonders where Boccaccio would place

[27]   Osgood, *Boccaccio on Poetry*, p. 94.
[28]   Ibid., p. 95.
[29]   Ibid., p. 96.
[30]   "Quis, inquit, has scenicas meretriculas ad hunc aegrum permisit accedere?" *De
consolatione philosophiae*, p. 68.
[31]   Osgood, p. 72.

himself as the author of a book dedicated to idle ladies and subtitled *Galeotto*. A passage in his *Esposizioni sopra la Comedia di Dante* composed around 1373 suggests how Boccaccio may be justified in exempting himself, as the author of the *Decameron*, from the category of bad poets. The writer returns to the opening pages of the *Consolatio* where he finds Boethius immobilized by self-pity:

> avendo per quello cacciata da sé ogni conoscenza del vero, non attendeva colla considerazione a trovare i rimedi opportuni a dover cacciar via le noie che danno gl'infortuni della presente vita; anzi cercava di comporre cose, le quali non liberasson lui, ma il mostrassero afflitto molto, e per conseguente mettessero compassion di lui in altrui. E questa gli pareva sì soave operazione che, senza guardare che egli in ciò faceva ingiuria alla filosofica verità; la ciu opera è di sanare, non di lusingare il passionato, che esso con la dolcezza delle lusinghe del potersi dolere insino alla sua estrema confusione avrebbe in tale impresa proceduto; e, pero chè questo è essercizio de' comici di sopra detti, a fine di guardagnare, di lusingare e di compiacere alle inferme menti, chiama la Filosofia queste muse "meretricule scenice," non perchè ella creda le Muse essere meretrici, ma per vituperare con questo vocabolo lo 'ngegno dell'artifice che nelle disoneste cose le 'nduce.[32]

This passage may be read as a gloss on a gloss, explaining some of the uncertainties generated by Boccaccio's exegesis of the distinction between the good and bad Muses presented earlier in his *De genealogia*. The malign influence of the comic Muses is now made explicit. They inspire Boethius to write verses which, failing to free him from pain, instead dramatize his suffering in order to elicit a predictable response from his public. Boethius is given permission to wallow in grief, and the resulting verses are exercises in self-pity, unproductive for the poet who must continually rehearse his wrongs, and for his readers whose response will be the perfunctory, and perhaps guilty, outpouring of compassion. In the process of exposing the comic Muses, Boccaccio gives us parenthetical insights into the operations of their better sisters—the handmaidens of Lady Philosophy who adorn her teaching with verse. Theirs is the task of healing sick minds, rather than pandering to them.

It is this theme of healing, traceable from Boethius to Petrarch to Boccaccio in his philological works, which exempts the *Decameron* from the category of bad poetry and identifies its inspiration with the likes of the better Muses. Storytelling is twice seen as the remedy for illness: when Boccaccio is cured by the fictions of his friend in the proem, and when the *brigata* reacts to the moral and physical perils of plague-ravaged Florence by telling tales in the country. But it would

---

[32] *Esposizioni sopra la Comedia di Dante*, p. 42.

be oversimplifying to say that all stories have the healing powers of the good Muses, for some indeed bespeak the maudlin self-indulgence of their lesser sisters. Within the *Decameron* itself, Boccaccio offers products of both the healing Muses who truly console, and those whose false consolation allows some of the defeatism of the outside world to seep into the closed confines of the pastoral retreat. The duality between healing and debilitating fictions is reflected in the uses and abuses of the term consolation throughout the text. The abuses of the term are frequent, and they take various forms, some of which will be considered in the following pages.

Though the standard dictionary definition of consolation, in Boccaccio's time as well as in our own, is the peace attendant upon the relief of psychic pain, there is a second definition, now obsolete, which occurs in the *Decameron* and suggests the opposition between the true and false consolation implicit in Boethius. Consolation, in this second sense, means the gratification of personal needs (often physical ones)[33] and hence reduces the original psychological and spiritual meaning of the term to the level of sensual pleasure. Thus, in the term "consolation," the Boethian ideal of self-transcendence coexists with its own most debased form—that of narcissistic attention to physical drives—an ambiguity which the rhetoric of courtly love shamelessly exploits. The alleviation of psychic pain through philosophical insights becomes, for the successful lover, the alleviation of sexual frustration in the embraces of his lady. This debased Boethian ideal recurs throughout the *Decameron* in the promises of love partners, like Madonna Beatrice (VII, 7) who tells her long-suffering suitor Anichino "ti consolerò di così lungo desio come avuto hai" (477), in the supplications of go-betweens like the handmaiden of Lidia in VII, 9 who begs Pirro to oblige her mistress ("io ti priego che ti piaccia di consolarla del suo disiderio" 489), in the intimation of a future of birdcatching for Ricciardo in V, 4 who with Caterina "in consolazione uccellò agli usignuoli e di dì e di notte quanto gli piacque" (361), in the countless consolations of Alatiel (II, 7) for her extinguished lovers, and in the nocturnal visits of the Angel Gabriel (IV, 2) "il quale di cielo in terra discende la notte a consolare le donne viniziane" (283). Examples of erotic consolation are legion in the *Decameron*, alerting us to the irony in Boccaccio's promise to comfort the idle ladies of his dedication.

Elsewhere the theme of consolation, though not sexualized, is nonetheless debased. Like the unfortunate Griselda, consolation itself

---

[33] "Consolare: appagare, compiacere, accontentare; anche: soddisfare (un bisogno fisico)." Boccaccio is among the authors cited who use the term in this way. See the *Grande dizionario della lingua italiana*, III (Turin, 1964), 607.

suffers at the hands of Gualtieri in X, 10. The first occurrence of the term in the story seems innocent enough, as the marquess chooses Griselda for his spouse, expecting to share with her "vita assai consolata" (704). But the term gains a sinister force when applied to Gualtieri's acquisition of psychic peace at so dear a cost to Griselda. Only after she has undergone over a decade of ordeals does Gualtieri consider himself consoled ("parendo a me aver di te quella consolazione che io desiderava" 711). In the closing line of the tale, this consolation is projected onto an indefinite future, "con Griselda, onorandola sempre quanto più si potea, lungamente e consolato visse" (712). Consolation is also ascribed to Giannucole, when Gualtieri finally sees fit to rescue his father-in-law from poverty, "che egli onoratamente e con gran consolazione visse" (712). Surprisingly, Griselda is never herself the beneficiary of that consolation attributed to the male protagonists, though it is she who endures the losses and is then restored to her former condition of plentitude. Instead, she is the agent of consolation for the others—the sacrificial victim on whom their psychic peace is founded. How far we have strayed from the Boethian ideal of consolation is obvious. Gualtieri's maniacal testing of his wife is a narcissistic compulsion to fulfill his own drive for power and only the continuous brutalizing of another human being will suffice to satisfy his needs. His is the opposite of Boethian consolation not only in its inhumanity, but in its lack of self-sufficiency. Gualtieri's gratification relies exclusively on another creature's willing abdication of the will, and his dependence is such that it requires repeated proofs of his sovereignty. When Dioneo labels Gualtieri's behavior "matta bestialità" (703), he reveals the distance between this power-hungry narcissism which passes for consolation, and the Boethian ideal which enlists those supremely human faculties of the mind and spirit.

False notions of consolation govern several subgenres of tales in the *Decameron*, particularly those of tragedy and romance. Day IV, for example, with its concentration on unhappy love, and with the consequent abdication of human control over destiny, according to the medieval definition of tragedy,[34] is a distinct threat to the equilibrium of the *Decameron* and must be duly exorcised. As discussed earlier,[35] the *brigata* seems to resent the imperative to tell sad stories, and two of the narrators, Pampinea and Dioneo, blatantly defy the dictates of

---

[34] The medieval definition of tragedy was an exceedingly simple one, involving none of the Aristotelian requirements of *hamartia*, catharsis, the laws of necessity and probability, and so on. See, for example, Dante's definition in his *Letter to Can Grande*. "Differt ergo a tragedia in materia per hoc, quod tragedia in principio est admirabilis et quieta, in fine seu exitu est fetida et horribilis," in *Tutte le opere*, p. 863.

[35] See Chapter III.

Filostrato, king for the day, by telling comic tales. In proposing the theme of tragic love for Day IV, Filostrato explains his selfish motive: "non d'altra materia domane mi piace che si ragioni se non di quello che a' miei fatti è più conforme, cioè di coloro li cui amori ebbero infelice fine" (256). This *brigata* member wants the stories told under his regime to reflect his own miserable situation, making Day IV a testament to pity for the unhappy youth.[36] In his self-indulgence, Filostrato anticipates the above-mentioned portrait of Boethius which Boccaccio gives us in his *Esposizioni sopra la Comedia di Dante*— imprisoned by his political enemies and also by the paralyzing demons of his own mind. Boccaccio's vision of the unregenerate Boethius, prey to all his worst instincts of defeatism and narcissistic self-involvement, offers a retrospective gloss on the character of Filostrato who insists on rehearsing his own troubles in order to exact pity from others. Like the unreclaimed Boethius, Filostrato "cercava di comporre cose, le quali non liberasson lui, ma il mostrassero afflitto molto e per conseguente mettessero compassion di lui in altrui." This self-dramatizing young man is engaging in the falsest of consolations, imposing his idea of catharsis through storytelling on a group which is of an entirely different mind. At last Filostrato himself recognizes the unpopularity of his theme when he apologizes for his gloom and suggests another, healthier form of consolation. In handing the crown to Fiammetta, he relents: "Io pongo a te questa corona sì come a colei la quale meglio dell'aspra giornata d'oggi, che alcuna altra, con quella di domane queste nostre compagne racconsolar saprai" (326). Indeed, there is another, better way to console, and that is comically, as Filostrato belatedly admits. But already within the confines of Day IV, the *brigata* has purged itself of tragic love. The last tale, Dioneo's, has already replaced the tears of the weeping listeners with laughter. "Se le prime novelle li petti delle vaghe donne avevano contristati, questa ultima di Dioneo le fece tanto ridere . . . che esse si poterono della compassione avuta dell'altre ristorare" (326). So even within Day IV, the *brigata* has shown its ability to restore a comic mood, to dispel the shadows of tragedy that Filostrato had selfishly cast upon them.

Just as tragedy must be expelled from the *Decameron*, so must the rule of fortune, for it too offers the promise of a false consolation in the rehearsal of the woes which befall mankind. In her preface to the tale of Madonna Beritola (II, 6), Emilia typifies the flawed approach of one who has yet to learn the lessons of Boethius. "Gravi cose e

---

[36] Joan Ferrante considers Filostrato an allegorical figure of despair or dread, and finds his choice of theme for Day IV a highly appropriate one. See "The Frame Characters of the *Decameron*," p. 220.

noiose sono i movimenti varii della fortuna, de' quali però che quante
volte alcuna cosa si parla, tante è un destare delle nostre menti, . . .
guidico mai rincrescer non dover l'ascoltare e a' felici e agli sventurati,
in quanto li primi rende avvisati e i secondi consola" (108). Emilia
offers to console those of us who are already in the throes of unhappiness with a story about the vicissitudes of fortune and the helplessness of men. We will be comforted because misery loves company and
we will be glad to see our own misfortunes objectified in art. Perhaps
we will be consoled because our own unhappiness will seem paltry
compared to our protagonists', or because we will be satisfied to see
misfortunes contained by an aesthetic form. But our consolation will
be illusory and self-defeating—we will not be given superior insight
into the operation of human affairs nor will we be shown an alternative to this vision of the world as arbitrary and uncontrollable.[37]

Emilia's bias in the preface to II, 6 is reminiscent of Boethius' own
flawed logic before undergoing the rigors of a course in philosophy.
He views himself as an undeserving victim of misfortune and is but a
short step from the position that the world is itself the thrall of ran-
dom governing forces. The entire thrust of Lady Philosophy's argument has been to persuade Boethius that he lives in an ordered
cosmos—one informed by a principle of justice to which the human
intellect may not always have access. Yet there is in Boethius another,
more modest solution to the question of man's place in the cosmos
and it is one which requires no recourse to superhuman explanations.
This is Lady Philosophy's imperative to mental and spiritual self-
sufficiency—a teaching of such importance to Boccaccio's proto-
humanist morality that it behooves us to dwell a moment on so fundamental an aspect of the *Consolatio*. Throughout the first three books
of the treatise, Boethius is told that he contains within his own mind
all the requisites for worldly satisfaction. "Why then do men look
outside themselves for happiness which is within?" (29). Lady
Philosophy's elegy on the Golden Age (p. 33) exemplifies that self-
sufficiency which made men satisfied with a diet of acorns and a bed
of grass, while worldly goods are discredited because they give the
illusion of fulfillment without its reality (pp. 47, 48, 57, 64). Lady
Philosophy uses this ideal as a standard against which she measures all
other alleged agents of happiness, since the perfect state is one in
which nothing is lacking. Accordingly, Boethius' guide embodies this
ideal in the very way in which she frames her discourse, giving cohe-

---

[37] Boccaccio dramatizes the same flawed perspective in another work, the *Fiammetta*,
where a long apostrophe to fortune reveals the lovesick heroine's sense of helplessness
in the face of frustration and loss. See *Opere minori*, ed. Enrico Bianchi (Florence, 1964),
pp. 145-146.

sion to the form and content of her teaching, as the prisoner himself observes: "And you proved all this without outside assumptions and used only internal proofs which draw their force from one another" (73). The absence of external explanations, and the mutually supportive relationship of the internal elements in her discourse make her logic the very paragon of the self-sufficiency she advocates. It is this organic unity between the form and the content of her plea which perfects Lady Philosophy's example.

The Boethian ideal of self-sufficiency operates on several textual levels in the *Decameron*. Most obvious is the decision of the *brigata* to abandon the city which represents the world of external goods in all its mutability, and to live in pastoral seclusion. The three villas of the fifteen-day sojourn are fitted with all the necessities of daily life, and the presence of servants means that the *brigata*'s physical comforts will be met by members of the immediate community. Pampinea's injunction to allow no bad news into the confines of the pastoral retreat enhances the autonomy of this vacation from the world of fortune and chance. It is the very process of storytelling, however, which best exemplifies the Boethian principle of consolation, for in the act of telling tales, the frame story youths affirm those inner resources of the mind which help them to defeat the paralysis of self-pity and despair overcome by Boethius with the help of Lady Philosophy. Here, a further definition of consolation comes to bear, subsuming and transcending the standard meanings in a final celebration of the Boethian ideal. To console means not only to satisfy physical needs and alleviate psychic pain, but it also means to restore or recreate the victim of loss.[38] In the case of Boethius, Lady Philosophy must recreate him in the etymological sense of the word, discrediting the false system of values to which he subscribes and starting from scratch in rebuilding a healthy mind and spirit. In this way the *Decameron*, too, consoles, for the *brigata* experiences true recreation in its storytelling venture. By leaving the horrors of the city behind, the young people build a narrative world, obedient this time not to the dictates of external fortune, but to the laws of reason and imagination. Boethius' withdrawal from dependence on false goods and the embrace of his own inner resources is thus recapitulated by the narrative experience of the *brigata* in the Tuscan countryside. But the withdrawal of prisoner and *brigata* is by no means total—the danger of a solipsistic *contemptus mundi* is scrupulously avoided by both writers. For each addresses his teachings to a public living within the world—a public whose inevitable dependence on the gifts of fortune may be thereby

[38] "Consolare: ristorare, ricreare, dar refrigerio, rincigorare, compensare." *Grande dizionario della lingua italiana*, III, 607.

rendered less absolute, and thus less dangerous. Boethius, in prison, and the *brigata*, in self-willed exile, view their cultures from a detached perspective whose beneficiaries will be those lacking in, yet desperately needing, such critical distance. History never allowed Boethius to reenter his society nor to deliver in person the gifts of his encounter with Lady Philosophy, but fiction allows the *Decameron* youths to return to the city, ready to bring the fruits of their narrative experience to bear on civic life. One critic cogently argues that Boccaccio posits a circular movement from city to country to city on every textual level of the *Decameron*, suggesting that the lessons learned in the natural world are meant to be applied in an urban context.[39] Thus, Boccaccio's didactic intent in telling stories is to affirm the social order at least, to reform and renew it at best.

The *Decameron* ends with a return to the proemial promise of consolation. In his conclusion, Boccaccio addresses his readers as "nobilissime giovani, a consolazion delle quali io a così lunga fatica messo mi sono" (717), echoing his introductory intention to comfort the lovelorn as he himself had been comforted by a sympathetic friend. But the theme of consolation has been infinitely enriched in the process of telling stories, once the debased constructions of the term have been explored and dismissed to make way for a truly consolatory mode of fiction-making. What started out as a simple balm for the heartsick has become an affirmation of the human resources for regeneration and hope—those faculties which allowed Boethius literally to recreate himself in the face of unspeakable loss, and the *brigata* to recreate a world in the wake of collective disaster.[40] When applied to Boccaccio, the sublime calm achieved by Boethius in the *Consolatio* may indeed justify the epithet *Johannes tranquillitatum*. Let this name, however, be understood in the Boethian sense of a tranquillity arising from an honest confrontation of moral issues, and not from an evasion of them, as Boccaccio critics have too often claimed. Let *Johannes tranquillitatum* be that Boccaccio who has welcomed the normative responsibilities of his art and composed a work of true consolation, dramatizing his faith in the human power to recreate the self and the world in the best tradition of Boethius.

---

[39] See Marga Cottino-Jones, "The City/Country Conflict in the *Decameron*," pp. 151, 155, 172, 183, in particular. Janet Smarr also remarks on the social implications of the *brigata*'s withdrawal and return to the city. See "Symmetry and Balance in the *Decameron*," p. 165.

[40] In his "Boccaccio's *Ars Narrandi*," Franco Fido argues that the *Decameron* is a cultural salvage operation, redeeming and ennobling what would otherwise be lost in the ravages of history. "That is why it is possible to envisage the *Decameron*, quite literally, as Boccaccio's answer to the plague" (240).

BIBLIOGRAPHY

Adriani, Maurilio. *Italia magica*. Rome, 1970.

Alighieri, Dante. *Tutte le opere*. Ed. Fredi Chiappelli. Milan, 1969.

Almansi, Guido. *The Writer as Liar: Narrative Technique in the 'Decameron.'* London, 1975.

Andreas Capellanus. *The Art of Courtly Love*. Trans. John Jay Parry. New York, 1969.

Aristotle. *The Works of Aristotle*. 12 vols. Ed. W.D. Ross. Oxford, 1908-1952.

Auerbach, Erich. *Mimesis: The Representation of Reality in Western Literature*. Trans. Willard R. Trask. Princeton, 1971.

Baldwin, Charles Sears. *Medieval Rhetoric and Poetic*. New York, 1928.

Baratto, Mario. *Realtà e stile nel 'Decameron.'* Vicenza, 1974.

Barilli, Renato. "Semiologia e retorica nella lettura del *Decameron*." *Verri*, 35-36 (1970), 27-48.

Battaglia, Salvatore. *La coscienza letteraria del medioevo*. Naples, 1965.

_____. *Giovanni Boccaccio e la riforma della narrativa*. Naples, 1969.

Berger, Harry. "L.B. Alberti on Painting: Art and Actuality in Humanist Perspective." *The Centennial Review*, 10 (1966), 237-277.

Billanovich, Giuseppe. *Restauri boccacceschi*. Rome, 1945.

Boccaccio, Giovanni. *Boccaccio on Poetry, Being the Preface and the Fourteenth and Fifteenth Books of Boccaccio's 'Genealogia Deorum Gentilium.'* Trans. Charles G. Osgood. New York, 1956.

_____. *Decameron, edizione critica secondo l'autografo hamiltoniano*. Ed. Vittore Branca. Florence: Accademia della Crusca, 1976.

_____. *Esposizioni sopra la Comedia di Dante* in *Tutte le opere di Giovanni Boccaccio*, VI. Ed. Giorgio Padoan. Milan, 1956.

_____. *Fiammetta* in *Opere minori*. Ed. Enrico Bianchi. Florence, 1964.

Boethius. *The Consolation of Philosophy*. Trans. Richard Green. Indianapolis and New York, 1962.

_____. *De consolatione philosophiae*. London, 1823.

Bonnet, Jules. *Vie d'Olympia Morata: Épisode de la renaissance et de la réforme en Italie*. Paris, 1850.

Borsellino, Nino. "*Decameron* come teatro," in *Rozzi e intronati: Esperienze e forme di teatro dal 'Decameron' al 'Candelaio.'* Rome, 1976, pp. 13-50.

Branca, Vittore. *Boccaccio medievale*. Florence, 1970.

Carducci, Giosuè. *Petrarca e Boccaccio, edizione nazionale delle opere di Giosuè Carducci*, XI. Bologna, 1962.

Cate, Wirt Armistead. "The Problem of the Origin of the Griselda Story." *Studies in Philology*, 29 (July 1932), 389-405.

Chiappelli, Fredi. "Sul linguaggio del Sannazzaro." *Vox romanica*, 13 (1953), 40-50.

Ciavolella, Massimo. "La tradizione dell'*aegritudo amoris* nel *Decameron*." *Giornale storico della letteratura italiana*, 147 (1970), 496-517.

Cioffari, Vincenzo. "The Conception of Fortune in the *Decameron*." *Italica*, 17 (1940), 129-137.

Clark, Susan, and Julian Wasserman. "*Decameron* II, 4: The Journey of the Hero." *Mediaevalia*, 3 (Fall 1977), 1-16.

Cottino-Jones, Marga. *An Anatomy of Boccaccio's Style*. Naples, 1968.

_____. "The City/Country Conflict in the *Decameron*." *Studi sul Boccaccio*, VIII. Florence, 1974, pp. 147-184.

_____. "Fabula vs. Figura: Another Interpretation of the Griselda Story." *The Decameron, A New Translation*. Ed. Mark Musa and Peter Bondanella. New York, 1977.

_____. "Magic and Superstition in Boccaccio's *Decameron*." *Italian Quarterly*, 18 (Spring 1975), 5-32.

_____. "The Mode and Structure of Tragedy in Boccaccio's *Decameron* (IV, 9)." *Italian Quarterly*, 11 (1967), 63-88.

Croce, Benedetto. "La novella di Andreuccio da Perugia" in *Storie e leggende napoletane*. Bari, 1959, pp. 45-84.

Curtius, Ernst Robert. *European Literature and the Latin Middle Ages*. Trans. Willard R. Trask. New York and Evanston, 1963.

Davis, Walter. "Boccaccio: The Implications of Binary Forn." Presented at the Thirteenth Annual Conference on Medieval Studies, Kalamazoo, Michigan, May 4, 1978.

Deligiorgis, Stavros. *Narrative Intellection in the 'Decameron.'* Iowa City, 1975.

De Sanctis, Francesco. *Storia della letteratura italiana*. Florence, 1965.

Faral, Edmond. *Les arts poétiques du XIIe et du XIIIe siècle*. Paris, 1924.

Ferguson, Margaret. "St. Augustine's.Region of Unlikeness: The Crossing of Exile and Language." *The Georgia Review*, 29 (Winter 1975), 842-864.

Ferrante, Joan M. "The Frame Characters of the *Decameron*: A Progression of Virtues." *Romance Philology*, 19 (November 1965), 212-226.

Fido, Franco. "Boccaccio's *Ars Narrandi* in the Sixth Day of the *Decameron*." *Italian Literature: Roots and Branches, Essays in Honor of Thomas Goddard Bergin*. Ed. Giose Rimanelli and Kenneth John Atchity. New Haven and London, 1976, pp. 225-242.

_____. "Dante, personaggio mancato del *Decameron*." *Le metamorfosi del centauro: Studi e letture da Boccaccio a Pirandello*. Rome, 1977, pp. 77-90.

_____. "Rhetoric and Semantics in the *Decameron*." *Yale Italian Studies*, 2 (Winter 1978), 1-12.

Frye, Northrop. *Anatomy of Criticism: Four Essays*. Princeton, 1973.

Fuchs, Leonard. *De historia stirpium commentarii insignes*. London, 1555.

Gerard, John. *The Herball or General History of Plants*. London, 1597.

Getto, Giovanni. *Vita di forme e forme di vita nel 'Decameron.'* Turin, 1958.

Givens, Azzurra B. *La dottrina d'amore nel Boccaccio*. Florence, 1968.

Grabher, Carlo. "Il culto del Boccaccio per Dante e alcuni aspetti delle sue opere dantesche." *Studi danteschi*, 30 (1951), 129-156.

Graf, Arturo. *Miti, leggende, e superstizioni del medio evo*. Turin, 1925.

Greene, Thomas. "Forms of Accommodation in the *Decameron*." *Italica*, 45 (1968), 297-313.

Griffith, Dudley David. *The Origin of the Griselda Story*. Seattle, 1931.

Hastings, R. *Nature and Reason in the 'Decameron.'* Manchester, 1975.

Hauvette, Henri. *Boccace: Étude biographique et littéraire*. Paris, 1914.

Hollander, Robert. *Boccaccio's Two Venuses*. New York, 1977.

Hortis, Attilio. *Studj sulle opere latine del Boccaccio*. Trieste, 1879.

Huizinga, J. *The Waning of the Middle Ages*. Trans. F. Hopman. Garden City, 1954.

Iser, Wolfgang. *The Implied Reader: Patterns of Communication in Prose Fiction from Bunyan to Beckett*. Baltimore, 1974.

Kermode, Frank. *The Sense of an Ending: Studies in the Theory of Fiction*. New York, 1975.

Layman, B.J. "Boccaccio's Paradigm of the Artist and His Art." *Italian Quarterly*, 13 (Winter 1970), 19-36.

Lee, A.C. *The 'Decameron': Its Sources and Analogues*. New York, 1966.

Lewis, C.S. *The Allegory of Love*. New York, 1972.

Lowes, John Livingston. "The Loveres Maladye of Hereos." *Modern Philology*, 11 (1913-1914), 490-546.

Lucente, Greg. "The Fortunate Fall of Andreuccio da Perugia." *Forum italicum*, 10, n. 4 (1976), 323-344.

Marti, M. "Per una metalettura del *Corbaccio*: Il ripudio di Fiammetta." *Giornale storico della letteratura italiana*, 153 (1976), 60-86.

Mazzacurati, Giancarlo. "Alatiel ovvero gli alibi del desiderio," *Forma e ideologia*. Naples, 1974, pp. 25-65.

Mazzotta, Giuseppe. "The *Decameron*: The Literal and the Allegorical." *Italian Quarterly*, 18 (Spring 1975), 53-73.

_____. "The *Decameron*: The Marginality of Literature." *University of Toronto Quarterly*, 42 (1972), 64-81.

Muscetta, Carlo. *Giovanni Boccaccio*. Bari, 1972.

_____. *Lettura militante*. Florence, 1953.

Nelson, Lowry Jr. "The Fictive Reader and Literary Self-Reflexiveness." *The Disciplines of Criticism*. Ed. Peter Demetz, Thomas Greene, and Lowry Nelson, Jr. New Haven, 1968, pp. 173-191.

Nelson, Robert J. "Ritual Reality, Tragic Imitation, Mythic Projection." *Diacritics*, 6 (Summer 1976), 41-48.

Neri, Ferdinando. "Il disegno ideale del *Decameron*." *Storia e poesia*. Turin, 1936, pp. 51-60.

New Catholic Encyclopedia. New York, 1967.

Novellino e conti del Duecento. Ed. Sebastiano Lo Nigro. Turin, 1968.

Padoan, Giorgio. "Mondo aristocratico e mondo comunale nell'ideologia e nell'arte di Giovanni Boccaccio." *Studi sul Boccaccio*, II. Florence, 1964, pp. 81-216.

The Palace of Pleasure: An Anthology of the Novella. Ed. Maurice Valency and Harry Levtow. New York, 1960.

Patch, H.R. *The Goddess Fortuna in Mediaeval Literature*. Cambridge, Mass., 1927.

_____. *The Tradition of Boethius*. New York, 1935.

Pennington, Kenneth. "A Note to *Decameron* VI, 7: The Wit of Madonna Filippa." *Speculum*, 52 (October 1977), 902-905.

Petrarch, Francis. "On Boccaccio's *Decameron* and the Story of Griselda." Trans. James Harvey Robinson and Henry Winchester Rolfe, in *The 'Decameron,' A New Translation* .Ed. Mark Musa and Peter Bondanella. New York, 1977, pp. 184-188.

_____. *Opere latine di Francesco Petrarca*. Ed. Antonietta Bufano. Turin, 1975.

Petronio, Giuseppe. "I volti del *Decameron*." *Boccaccio: Secoli di vita, Atti del Congresso Internazionale, Boccaccio 1975*. Ed. Marga Cottino-Jones and Edward F. Tuttle. Ravenna, 1977, pp. 107-124.

Plinius Secundus, C. *The Natural History of Pliny*. 6 vols. Trans. John Bostock and H.T. Riley. London, 1855-1857.

Potter, Joy Hambuechen. "Boccaccio as Illusionist: The Play of Frames in the *Decameron*." *Humanities Association Review*, 26 (Fall 1975), 327-345.

Rajna, Pio. "Il titolo del poema dantesco." *Studi danteschi*, 4 (1921), 5-37.

Ramat, Raffaello. *Saggi sul rinascimento*. Florence, 1969.

Ricci, Pier Giorgio. "Dante e Boccaccio." *Alighieri*, 16, i-ii (1975), 75-84.

Ripa, Cesare. *Iconologia*. Padua, 1611.

Robertson, D.W. *A Preface to Chaucer: Studies in Medieval Perspectives*. Princeton, 1973.

Rossi, Aldo. "La combinatoria decameroniana: Andreuccio." *Strumenti critici*, 7 (February 1973), 1-51.

_____. "Dante nella prospettiva del Boccaccio." *Studi danteschi*, 37 (1960), 63-139.

Russo, Luigi. *Il Decameron*. Florence, 1939.

Russo, Vittorio. "Il senso del tragico nel *Decameron*." *Filologia e letteratura*, 11 (1965), 29-83.

Rutter, Itala Tania. "The Function of Dioneo's Perspective in the Griselda Story." *Comitatus*, 5 (1974), 33-42.

Sacchetti, Franco. *Trecentonovelle*. Ed. Vincenzo Pernicone. Florence, 1946.

Salinari, Carlo. "L'empirismo ideologico del Boccaccio." *La critica della letteratura italiana* .Ed. Carlo Salinari. Naples, 1973, pp. 363-370.

Sapegno, Natalino. *Il Trecento*. Milan, 1934.

Scaglione, Aldo. *Nature and Love in the Late Middle Ages*. Berkeley and Los Angeles, 1963.

Schiaffini, Alfredo. *Tradizione e poesia nella prosa d'arte italiana dalla latinità medievale a Giovanni Boccaccio*. Genoa, 1934.

Segre, Cesare. "Da Boccaccio a Lope de Vega." *Boccaccio: Secoli di vita, Atti del Congresso Internazionale, Boccaccio 1975*. Ed. Marga Cottino-Jones and Edward F. Tuttle. Ravenna, 1977.

_____. "Funzioni, opposizioni e simmetrie nella Giornata VII del *Decameron*." *Studi sul Boccaccio*, VI. Florence, 1971, pp. 81-108.

Seung, T.K. *Cultural Thematics: The Formation of the Faustian Ethos*. New Haven, 1976.

Singleton, Charles S. "On Meaning in the *Decameron*." *Italica*, 21 (1944), 117-124.

Šklovsky, V. "La construction de la nouvelle et du roman." *Théorie de la littérature: Textes des formalistes russes*. Ed. Tzvetan Todorov. Paris, 1965, pp. 170-196.

_____. *Lettura del 'Decameron': Dal romanzo d'avventura al romanzo di carattere*. Trans. Alessandro Ivanov. Bologna, 1969.

Smarr, Janet. "Symmetry and Balance in the *Decameron*." *Mediaevalia*, 2 (1976), 159-187.

Spitzer, Leo. *Linguistics and Literary History*. Princeton, 1948.

Stäuble, Antonio. "La brigata del *Decameron* come pubblico teatrale." *Studi sul Boccaccio*, IX (Florence, 1975-1976), 103-117.

Tateo, Francesco. "Il 'realismo' nella novella boccaccesca." *Retorica e poetica fra medievo e rinascimento*. Bari, 1960, pp. 197-202.

Theophrastus. *Enquiry into Plants*. 2 vols. Trans. Sir Arthur Holt. London, 1916.

Thorndike, Lynn. *A History of Magic and Experimental Science*. 8 vols. New York, 1923-1958.

Todorov, Tzvetan. *Grammaire du 'Décaméron.'* The Hague, 1969.

Vinaver, Eugene. *The Rise of Romance*. New York and Oxford, 1971.

Wimsatt, James. "Medieval and Modern in Chaucer's *Troilus and Criseyde*." *PMLA*, 92 (March 1977), 203-216.

INDEX*

Abraam (I, 2) 19 and n
Abruzzi 72, 84
Adriani, Maurilio 103
aegritudo amoris 114 and n
Alatiel (II, 7) 28, 35, 39-43, 120
Alberto (frate, IV, 2) 55
Alexandria 33
Alexandria, Egypt 41
Algarve 39, 41
Alighieri, Dante 1, 2, 21 and n, 24, 38, 48, 53, 82, 83, 96, 98, 108, 110-112, 121n
allegorical 5 and n, 7, 76, 97, 98
allegorist 4
allegory 5, 6, 9, 98, 99, 108
Almansi, Guido 3, 4 and n, 15n, 16 and n, 23, 47 and n, 53, 54n, 59 and n, 64 and n, 79n
Amorosa visione 112n
Andreas Capellanus 32n, 33, 46 and n, 47
Andreuccio da Perugia (II, 5) 28, 35-39, 42, 43, 115
Anichino (VII, 7) 120
Antigono (II, 7) 41
Antonio (santo) 65, 68
Antwerp 35
Ardji Bardji 114
Aristotelian 42
Aristotle 95 and n

Arrighetto Capece (II, 6) 29, 30, 31, 35, 43
Ars amatoria 118
Athens 40
Auerbach, Erich 1 and n, 2 and n, 3, 24, 25n, 48n, 62 and n
Augustine 75n, 77n

Baldwin, Charles 70n
Baratto, Mario 8n, 19n, 39n, 45n, 47n, 49n, 50n, 53n, 72n, 81n, 91n
Barilli, Renato 8n
Baronci (VI, 5) 65
Battaglia, Salvatore 2 and n, 11 and n, 79n, 101n
Beatrice (VII, 7) 120
Benevento 29, 30
Bengodi 84, 85, 87
Bergamino (I, 7) 27
Berger, Harry 112n
Bergin, Thomas v, 8n
Beritola (II, 6) 28-35, 42, 43, 122
Betto Brunelleschi (VI, 9) 67, 68
Billanovich, Giuseppe 104n
Bito 81
Black Death 114
Boethius 38, 112-125
Bondanella, Peter 98n, 100n
Bonnet, Jules 19n
Borsellino, Nino 8n, 21n, 72n, 77n,

*Neither the name Boccaccio, nor the title *Decameron* have been indexed. Characters in the *Decameron* are listed by first names.

131

DATE DUE

MAR 0 9 2004		
MAR 2 9 2004		
MAR 2 7 2005		
MAR 0 5 2005		
JAN 1 6 2007		
JUN 0 8 2007		
FEB 1 5 2012		

GAYLORD

PRINTED IN U.S.A.

LAST COPY

COLUMBIA UNIVERSITY LIBRARIES

0045035903

STANFORD FRENCH AND ITALIAN STUDIES

Editor: *Alphonse Juilland*